VOICES
HEARING GOD IN A WORLD OF IMPOSTORS

New Testament

by

pam gillaspie

**Voices: Hearing God in a World of
Impostors, Old Testament**

Copyright © 2025 by Pam Gillaspie

Ignite Bible Ministries

www.pamgillaspie.com

ISBN 978-1-960938-12-1

Printed in the United States of America

2025

VOICES
HEARING GOD
IN A WORLD OF
IMPOSTORS

New Testament

Dedication

This study is dedicated to the bride of Christ, the Church. In these last days as it
becomes harder and harder to stand on truth, may you cling to the Word of God
and live boldly by the power of the Spirit.

VOICES
HEARING GOD
IN A WORLD OF
IMPOSTORS

There is nothing quite like your favorite pair of jeans. You can dress them up, you can dress them down. You can work in them, play in them, shop in them . . . live in them. They always feel right. It is my hope that the structure of this Bible study will fit you like those jeans; that it will work with your life right now, right where you are whether you're new to this whole Bible thing or whether you've been studying the Book for years!

How is this even possible? Smoke and mirrors, perhaps? The new mercilessly thrown in the deep end? The experienced given pompoms and the job of simply cheering others on? None of the above.

Flexible inductive Bible studies are designed with options that will allow you to go as deep each week as you desire. If you're just starting out and feeling a little overwhelmed, stick with the main text and don't think a second thought about the sidebar assignments. If you're looking for a challenge, then take the sidebar prompts and go ahead and dig all the way to China! As you move along through the study, think of the sidebars and "Digging Deeper" boxes as that 2% of lycra that you find in certain jeans . . . the wiggle-room that will help them fit just right.

Beginners may find that they want to start adding in some of the optional assignments as they go along. Experts may find that when three children are throwing up for three days straight, foregoing those assignments for the week is the way to live wisely.

Life has a way of ebbing and flowing and this study is designed to ebb and flow right along with it!

Enjoy!

HOW TO USE THIS STUDY

Flexible inductive Bible studies meet you where you are and take you as far as you want to go.

1. WEEKLY STUDY: The main text guides you through the complete topic of study for the week.

2. FYI boxes: For Your Information boxes provide bite-sized material to shed additional light on the topic.

> **FYI:**
>
> **Reading Tip: Begin with prayer**
> You may have heard this a million times over and if this is a million and one, so be it. Whenever you read or study God's Word, first pray and ask His Spirit to be your Guide.

3. ONE STEP FURTHER and other sidebar boxes: Sidebar boxes give you the option to push yourself a little further. If you have extra time or are looking for an extra challenge, you can try one, all, or any number in between! These boxes give you the ultimate in flexibility.

> **ONE STEP FURTHER:**
>
> **Word Study: _torah_/law**
> The first of eight Hebrew key words we encounter for God's Word is _torah_ translated "law." If you're up for a challenge this week, do a word study to learn what you can about _torah_. Run a concordance search and examine where the word _torah_ appears in the Old Testament and see what you can learn from the contexts.
>
> If you decide to look for the word for "law" in the New Testament, you'll find that the primary Greek word is _nomos_.
>
> Be sure to see what Paul says about the law in Galatians 3 and what Jesus says in Matthew 5.

4. DIGGING DEEPER boxes: If you're looking to go further, Digging Deeper sections will help you sharpen your skills as you continue to mine the truths of Scripture for yourself.

> **Digging Deeper**
>
> **What else does God's Word say about counselors?**
>
> If you can, spend some time this week digging around for what God's Word says about counselors.
>
> Start by considering what you already know about counsel from the Word of God and see if you can actually show where these truths are in the Bible. Make sure that the Word actually says what you think it says.

WEEK ONE

Who Will You Listen To?

*"For false Christs and false prophets will arise and will show great
signs and wonders, so as to mislead, if possible, even the elect.
Behold, I have told you in advance."*
—Jesus
Matthew 24:24-25

Has any time in history been as loud as ours? More voices call from more
directions with more conflicting words than ever before. In a world of sensational
spiritual claims, when do we listen and when do we just say "No!"? It's time to stop
wondering and start discovering biblical answers. Over the next eight weeks, we'll
look at the New Testament to discover how God communicates with His people
and with others so we can learn to discern and stand firm in an age marked by
radical deception.

FYI:

If You're in a Class

Complete **Week One** together on your
first day of class. This will be a great way
to start getting to know one another and
it will help those who are newer to Bible
study get their bearings.

VOICES
HEARING GOD
IN A WORLD OF
IMPOSTORS

New Testament

Week One: **Who Will You Listen To?**

REVIEW for those who have taken *Voices: Old Testament*

(If this is your first *Voices* class, skip ahead to the next section!)

How did God speak during Old Testament times?

What types of people did He speak to?

What, if any, recurring patterns did you notice?

What was your biggest takeaway from studying how God spoke during Old Testament times?

What is your biggest question as we move into the New Testament portion of our study?

CONSIDER the WAY you THINK

As we start our study, we need to examine our presuppositions and define terms. For now, let's consider what views we're bringing to the table.

How do you think God speaks today? Why do you believe this?

If someone said "God told me . . ." how would you respond?

VOICES
HEARING GOD
IN A WORLD OF
IMPOSTORS

New Testament

What is your view on the authority of Scripture? What about the sufficiency of Scripture?

A DRAMATIC SHIFT

As we move into the New Testament portion of our study, we need to be aware that the Word itself talks about a shift that has taken place in how God speaks. Before we jump into the Gospel accounts, let's look briefly at the opening words of the book of Hebrews as we start our New Testament journey together.

OBSERVE the TEXT of SCRIPTURE

READ Hebrews 1:1-2 and **MARK** the words *spoke/spoken*.

Hebrews 1:1-2

1 *God, after He spoke long ago to the fathers in the prophets in many portions and in many ways,*

2 *in these last days has spoken to us in His Son, whom He appointed heir of all things, through whom also He made the world.*

DISCUSS with your GROUP or PONDER on your own . . .

How did God speak "long ago"? Who did He speak to? If you can, give some specific Old Testament examples.

How has God spoken "in these last days"? Is there any ambiguity in the statement?

The Days Before the Son

The Old Testament records mankind's history before the incarnation of God's Son and the early pages of the Gospel accounts do, too. During that time—prior to Jesus' birth and well before the Holy Spirit was poured out at Pentecost—God announced the Good News of the coming Savior.

FYI:

Dating the Book of Hebrews
The book of Hebrews dates to the first century AD. Because of the volume of references to the sacrificial system—which seems to be in effect at the time of writing—the date is almost certainly prior to the destruction of the temple by Titus in AD70. While the days of Christ may be "long ago" to us, to the author of Hebrews' "long ago" refers back to Old Testament times.

ONE STEP FURTHER:

Watch the Verb Tenses
What verb tense does the author of Hebrews use for "spoke" and "has spoken"? What is significant about it? Why does it matter? Record your findings below.

VOICES
HEARING GOD
IN A WORLD OF
IMPOSTORS

New Testament 5

SETTING the SCENE

Before God sent word to either Mary or Joseph about Jesus, He sent an angel to an old priest with another message.

OBSERVE the TEXT of SCRIPTURE

READ Luke 1:5-20. **MARK** every reference to the *angel* including pronouns.

Luke 1:5-20

5 In the days of Herod, king of Judea, there was a priest named Zacharias, of the division of Abijah; and he had a wife from the daughters of Aaron, and her name was Elizabeth.

6 They were both righteous in the sight of God, walking blamelessly in all the commandments and requirements of the Lord.

7 But they had no child, because Elizabeth was barren, and they were both advanced in years.

8 Now it happened that while he was performing his priestly service before God in the appointed order of his division,

9 according to the custom of the priestly office, he was chosen by lot to enter the temple of the Lord and burn incense.

10 And the whole multitude of the people were in prayer outside at the hour of the incense offering.

11 And an angel of the Lord appeared to him, standing to the right of the altar of incense.

12 Zacharias was troubled when he saw the angel, and fear gripped him.

13 But the angel said to him, "Do not be afraid, Zacharias, for your petition has been heard, and your wife Elizabeth will bear you a son, and you will give him the name John.

14 "You will have joy and gladness, and many will rejoice at his birth.

15 "For he will be great in the sight of the Lord; and he will drink no wine or liquor, and he will be filled with the Holy Spirit while yet in his mother's womb.

16 "And he will turn many of the sons of Israel back to the Lord their God.

17 "It is he who will go as a forerunner before Him in the spirit and power of Elijah, TO TURN THE HEARTS OF THE FATHERS BACK TO THE CHILDREN, and the disobedient to the attitude of the righteous, so as to make ready a people prepared for the Lord."

18 Zacharias said to the angel, "How will I know this for certain? For I am an old man and my wife is advanced in years."

19 The angel answered and said to him, "I am Gabriel, who stands in the presence of God, and I have been sent to speak to you and to bring you this good news.

FYI:

Luke's Record

Matthew, Mark, and Luke are often referred to as the Synoptic Gospels. These record the life and times of Jesus in a linear fashion unlike John who structures his Gospel account thematically. Luke's record is distinct from the other two, however, in its pre-birth focus on Gabriel's revelations to Zacharias and Mary. Mark opens with Jesus as an adult while Matthew focuses on God's dealings with Joseph.

ONE STEP FURTHER:

Malachi 4

Luke 1:17 quotes from the prophet Malachi. If you have extra time this week, read this short chapter that closes the Old Testament and record your observations of the original prophecy below.

20 *"And behold, you shall be silent and unable to speak until the day when these things take place, because you did not believe my words, which will be fulfilled in their proper time."*

DISCUSS with your GROUP or PONDER on your own . . .

Briefly describe Zacharias.

What is Zacharias doing when the angel appears to him? How did he end up being there?

How does he respond when the angel appears to him? What emotion hit him?

What does the angel tell Zacharias? (Stick to the text.)

How does Zacharias respond to the angel's words? What happens as a result? How does this authenticate the message short-term?

Based on verses 16-17, what will the prophesied child do? How will this relate to the Messiah?

INDUCTIVE FOCUS:

Listing What You Learn

Making lists of significant information is an inductive Bible study skill that helps us observe the text well. If you have time this week, list everything you learned about Zacharias and Elizabeth in Luke 1:5-20.

Zacharias

Elizabeth

Considering the whole passage, why does the angel come to Zacharias? Is it just a response to a personal request or something more? How does it fit into God's big picture and plan? Explain.

How clear are the prophecies? How many are empirically verifiable? Is there any call to action?

ONE STEP FURTHER:

Filled with the Spirit

While the angel Gabriel speaks directly to both Zacharias and Mary, the broader text (up to v. 67) describes two people, John and Zacharias, "filled with the Spirit" and prophesying (pre-Pentecost). If you have some time this week, look into these accounts and see what you can discover. Record your findings below.

The Rest of the Story

John the Baptist, who appears in each of the four Gospel accounts, fulfills the prophecy Gabriel made to Zacharias. Born to an old priest and his long-barren wife, John is the prophesied messenger who will prepare the Lord's way.

SETTING the SCENE

Zacharias isn't the only person who encounters Gabriel. The angel sent to bring news of a son to Zacharias in the temple is sent shortly thereafter to bring news of another Son to Mary in Nazareth.

OBSERVE the TEXT of SCRIPTURE

READ Luke 1:26-38 and **MARK** every reference to the *angel* and to *Mary*.

Luke 1:26-38

26 *Now in the sixth month the angel Gabriel was sent from God to a city in Galilee called Nazareth,*

27 *to a virgin engaged to a man whose name was Joseph, of the descendants of David; and the virgin's name was Mary.*

28 *And coming in, he said to her, "Greetings, favored one! The Lord is with you."*

29 *But she was very perplexed at this statement, and kept pondering what kind of salutation this was.*

30 *The angel said to her, "Do not be afraid, Mary; for you have found favor with God.*

31 *"And behold, you will conceive in your womb and bear a son, and you shall name Him Jesus.*

32 *"He will be great and will be called the Son of the Most High; and the Lord God will give Him the throne of His father David;*

33 and He will reign over the house of Jacob forever, and His kingdom will have no end."

34 Mary said to the angel, "How can this be, since I am a virgin?"

35 The angel answered and said to her, "The Holy Spirit will come upon you, and the power of the Most High will overshadow you; and for that reason the holy Child shall be called the Son of God.

36 "And behold, even your relative Elizabeth has also conceived a son in her old age; and she who was called barren is now in her sixth month.

37 "For nothing will be impossible with God."

38 And Mary said, "Behold, the bondslave of the Lord; may it be done to me according to your word." And the angel departed from her.

DISCUSS with your GROUP or PONDER on your own . . .

Briefly describe Mary.

How does Gabriel address Mary? What message from God does he bring to her?

What will this Son be called? What will He do?

What does Mary ask? How does the angel answer her? What evidence does He give her that God can do these things?

Again, reviewing the entire passage, why did God send the angel? Was it just a personal matter or something more? Explain.

INDUCTIVE FOCUS:

Marking the Text
Marking the text is a simple way to help see key words. When marking one word, a circle, underline, or highlight works great. If you decide to mark multiple words in a passage of Scripture, you may choose to use different colored pencils, symbols, or a combination of the two.

VOICES
HEARING GOD
IN A WORLD OF
IMPOSTORS

How many promises were quickly fulfilled and thus quickly verified? Was there any call to action?

ONE STEP FURTHER:

Other Prophecies Fulfilled

If you have some extra time this week, compile a list of Old Testament prophecies Jesus fulfilled. Sure, you could Google it, but don't. Instead take some time to think through what you know of the biblical text and see how you can do on your own. There are hundreds to find, so be careful not to spend *all* your homework time working on this sidebar assignment, but do take the opportunity to stretch your brain across the pages of Scripture to start tying some of the threads together on your own! Compiling a list from Google will be boring; piecing it together from what you've already learned will be gratifying!

The Rest of the Story

Mary goes to see the formerly barren Elizabeth who, the angel said, was already in her sixth month of pregnancy (with John the Baptist). She eventually conceives and bears Jesus, the promised Messiah, exactly the way the angel had foretold.

SETTING the SCENE

Luke recounts the first two direct messages from God that people received during New Testament times. The angel Gabriel delivered both, one as we've seen to Zacharias, the other to Mary. God's message to Joseph takes place later and has some distinctive features. Let's take a look.

OBSERVE the TEXT of SCRIPTURE

READ Matthew 1:18-25 and **MARK** every reference to *angel*. **UNDERLINE** any sleep-related words (*dream, awoke, sleep*).

Matthew 1:18-25

18 *Now the birth of Jesus Christ was as follows: when His mother Mary had been betrothed to Joseph, before they came together she was found to be with child by the Holy Spirit.*

19 *And Joseph her husband, being a righteous man and not wanting to disgrace her, planned to send her away secretly.*

20 *But when he had considered this, behold, an angel of the Lord appeared to him in a dream, saying, "Joseph, son of David, do not be afraid to take Mary as your wife; for the Child who has been conceived in her is of the Holy Spirit.*

21 *"She will bear a Son; and you shall call His name Jesus, for He will save His people from their sins."*

22 *Now all this took place to fulfill what was spoken by the Lord through the prophet:*

23 *"BEHOLD, THE VIRGIN SHALL BE WITH CHILD AND SHALL BEAR A SON, AND THEY SHALL CALL HIS NAME IMMANUEL," which translated means, "GOD WITH US."*

24 *And Joseph awoke from his sleep and did as the angel of the Lord commanded him, and took Mary as his wife,*

25 *but kept her a virgin until she gave birth to a Son; and he called His name Jesus.*

DISCUSS with your GROUP or PONDER on your own . . .

According to verse 19, what is Joseph planning and why?

When does the angel of the Lord appear to Joseph? What are the circumstances?

How does this appearance differ from the appearances to Zacharias and Mary? How is it similar?

What counsel does the angel bring? What information does he give?

How does this message compare to those given to Mary and Zacharias?

Again, reviewing the entire passage, why does God send the angel? Is t just a personal matter or something more? Explain.

Mid-Way Recap . . .

Consider the overall similarities and differences in the ways God communicated with Zacharias, Mary, and Joseph. How quickly did each one align their thinking with God's? Do you quickly align your thinking with God's revealed Word in Scripture? Why and why not? (i.e. explain both your promptnesses and delays.)

VOICES
HEARING GOD
IN A WORLD OF
IMPOSTORS

SETTING the SCENE

Unlike anyone else who has ever lived, Jesus enters the world with an amazing symphony of pre-announcements:

• the Old Testament Scriptures prophesy His coming.

• the angel Gabriel announces to Zacharias the birth of the one who will be His herald.

• the angel Gabriel announces to Mary that she will conceive a Child by the Holy Spirit.

• the angel of the Lord appears to Joseph in a dream and confirms what Mary has told him.

In our next collection of texts, we'll read about the various voices Scripture records after Christ's birth.

OBSERVE the TEXT of SCRIPTURE

READ Luke 2:8-20 and **MARK** in a distinctive way every reference to *angels* and *shepherds* including pronouns. Also **MARK** every occurrence of *Lord*.

Luke 2:8-20

8 In the same region there were some *shepherds staying out in the fields and keeping watch over their flock by night.*

9 And an *angel of the Lord suddenly stood before them,* and the glory of the *Lord shone around them; and they were terribly frightened.*

10 But the *angel said to them,* "Do not be afraid; for behold, *I bring you good news of great joy which will be for all the people;*

11 for today in the city of David there has been born for you a Savior, who is Christ the *Lord.*

12 "This will be *a sign for you: you will find a baby wrapped in cloths and lying in a manger."*

13 And suddenly there appeared with the *angel a multitude of the heavenly host praising God and saying,*

14 "Glory to God in the highest,   And on earth peace among men with whom He is pleased."

15 When the *angels had gone away from them into heaven, the shepherds began saying to one another, "Let us go straight to Bethlehem then, and see this thing that has happened which the Lord has made known to us."*

16 So *they came in a hurry and found their way to Mary and Joseph, and the baby as He lay in the manger.*

17 When *they had seen this, they made known the statement which had been told them about this Child.*

18 And all who heard it wondered at the things which were told them by the *shepherds.*

19 But Mary treasured all these things, pondering them in her heart.

---

20 *The shepherds went back, glorifying and praising God for all that they had heard and seen, just as had been told them.*

DISCUSS with your GROUP or PONDER on your own . . .

Who are the main characters in this section?

Describe the angel. What does he do? What message does he bring? Who is it for?

In what ways is the angel's message authenticated?

Using your marking of the word "Lord" as your guide, make a list of everything the text says about the "Lord."

Does "Lord" refer to more than one person in this passage? Explain.

Describe the shepherds. How do they respond to the angel and his message?

What do they do about it? What long-term effect does it have on them? On others?

What effect has it had on you? Is this message one we can still share today?

FYI:

The Lord has said to my Lord

"What do you think about the Christ, whose son is He?" They said to Him, "*The son* of David." He said to them, "Then how does David in the Spirit call Him 'Lord,' saying, 'THE LORD SAID TO MY LORD, "SIT AT MY RIGHT HAND, UNTIL I PUT YOUR ENEMIES BENEATH YOUR FEET"'? "If David then calls Him 'Lord,' how is He his son?"

—Matthew 22:42–45 (Cf. Psalm 110:1)

VOICES
HEARING GOD
IN A WORLD OF
IMPOSTORS

Digging Deeper

Start Reading through the Gospels

During our first two lessons we'll cover the Gospel accounts of people who heard from God. You'll get the most out of the study, though, if you lock in on the context and the entire narrative. This doesn't happen overnight. It takes time. If you have the time, read or listen to the Gospels of Matthew and Mark this week. Next week we'll have a Digging Deeper on Luke and John. As you read or listen, jot down the instances you note of God speaking to people and the contexts in which they happen.

Observations on Matthew:

Observations on Mark:

SETTING the SCENE

When Mary and Joseph bring the infant Jesus to the temple, they hear about yet another message that had come about Jesus prior to His birth.

OBSERVE the TEXT of SCRIPTURE

READ Luke 2:21-35 and **MARK** every reference to *Jesus* (include phrases used to describe Him). Also **MARK** every reference to the *Holy Spirit*.

Luke 2:21-35

21 *And when eight days had passed, before His circumcision, His name was then called Jesus, the name given by the angel before He was conceived in the womb.*

22 *And when the days for their purification according to the law of Moses were completed, they brought Him up to Jerusalem to present Him to the Lord*

23 *(as it is written in the Law of the Lord, "EVERY firstborn MALE THAT OPENS THE WOMB SHALL BE CALLED HOLY TO THE LORD"),*

24 and to offer a sacrifice according to what was said in the Law of the Lord, "A PAIR OF TURTLEDOVES OR TWO YOUNG PIGEONS."

25 And there was a man in Jerusalem whose name was Simeon; and this man was righteous and devout, looking for the consolation of Israel; and the Holy Spirit was upon him.

26 And it had been revealed to him by the Holy Spirit that he would not see death before he had seen the Lord's Christ.

27 And he came in the Spirit into the temple; and when the parents brought in the child Jesus, to carry out for Him the custom of the Law,

28 then he took Him into his arms, and blessed God, and said,

29 "Now Lord, You are releasing Your bond-servant to depart in peace,

According to Your word;

30 For my eyes have seen Your salvation,

31 Which You have prepared in the presence of all peoples,

32 A LIGHT OF REVELATION TO THE GENTILES,

And the glory of Your people Israel."

33 And His father and mother were amazed at the things which were being said about Him.

34 And Simeon blessed them and said to Mary His mother, "Behold, this Child is appointed for the fall and rise of many in Israel, and for a sign to be opposed—

35 and a sword will pierce even your own soul—to the end that thoughts from many hearts may be revealed."

DISCUSS with your GROUP or PONDER on your own . . .

When is Jesus brought to Jerusalem? What do the texts say?

What do Mary and Joseph do according to the Law of Moses?

Who is Simeon? What does he know? How does he know it?

ONE STEP FURTHER:

Word Study: Consolation

The Greek word translated "consolation" in Luke 2:25 may surprise you. If you have some extra time this week, find the corresponding Greek term (you can use its Strong's number) and see where else and how else it is used in the New Testament. Record your findings below.

ONE STEP FURTHER:

Word Study: "had been revealed"

If you have some extra time this week, find the Greek word that translates the phrase "had been revealed" in Luke 2:26. Once you've found the word, note what kind of verb you've found and see where else it shows up and how it is used elsewhere in the New Testament. Record your findings below.

VOICES
HEARING GOD
IN A WORLD OF
IMPOSTORS

Week One: **Who Will You Listen To?**

How is this account distinct from the others we looked at?

What phrases does Simeon use to describe Jesus? According to 1 Samuel 15:29 who is the glory of Israel? According to Isaiah 43:11—and other texts—who is the salvation of Israel?

Briefly recount Simeon's message and Mary and Joseph's response.

SETTING the SCENE

Following directly on the heels of the account about Simeon, Luke introduces us to a woman who confirms the old man's words.

OBSERVE the TEXT of SCRIPTURE

READ Luke 2:36-38 and **MARK** every reference to *Anna* including pronouns. Also **MARK** all time-related phrases that help answer the inductive question *"When?"*

Luke 2:36-38

36 *And there was a prophetess, Anna the daughter of Phanuel, of the tribe of Asher. She was advanced in years and had lived with her husband seven years after her marriage,*

37 *and then as a widow to the age of eighty-four. She never left the temple, serving night and day with fastings and prayers.*

38 *At that very moment she came up and began giving thanks to God, and continued to speak of Him to all those who were looking for the redemption of Jerusalem.*

DISCUSS with your GROUP or PONDER on your own . . .

Describe Anna. What is she like? What does she do?

FYI:

Repetition, Authentication, Confirmation

As we study, continue to keep your eyes open for the ways that God repeats, authenticates, and confirms His messages. Nothing is spoken in a vacuum.

Look closely at the time-related phrases. How long does she speak about Jesus and to who?

How do her words compare and relate to Simeon's? Why is this significant to Mary and Joseph? To us?

SETTING the SCENE

Although the magi stand alongside the shepherds in many nativity scenes and movies, the men from the east were later visitors to the Christ child and His family. *"Where?"* is a major question in this section.

OBSERVE the TEXT of SCRIPTURE

READ Matthew 2:1-12 and **MARK** every reference to *the star* and to *the magi*. Also **MARK** references to location that help answer *"Where?"*

Matthew 2:1-12

1 *Now after Jesus was born in Bethlehem of Judea in the days of Herod the king, magi from the east arrived in Jerusalem, saying,*

2 *"Where is He who has been born King of the Jews? For we saw His star in the east and have come to worship Him."*

3 *When Herod the king heard this, he was troubled, and all Jerusalem with him.*

4 *Gathering together all the chief priests and scribes of the people, he inquired of them where the Messiah was to be born.*

5 *They said to him, "In Bethlehem of Judea; for this is what has been written by the prophet:*

6 *'AND YOU, BETHLEHEM, LAND OF JUDAH,*

ARE BY NO MEANS LEAST AMONG THE LEADERS OF JUDAH;

FOR OUT OF YOU SHALL COME FORTH A RULER

WHO WILL SHEPHERD MY PEOPLE ISRAEL.' "

7 *Then Herod secretly called the magi and determined from them the exact time the star appeared.*

8 *And he sent them to Bethlehem and said, "Go and search carefully for the Child; and when you have found Him, report to me, so that I too may come and worship Him."*

9 *After hearing the king, they went their way; and the star, which they had seen in the east, went on before them until it came and stood over* the place *where the Child was.*

10 *When they saw the star, they rejoiced exceedingly with great joy.*

11 *After coming into the house they saw the Child with Mary His mother; and they fell to the ground and worshiped Him. Then, opening their treasures, they presented to Him gifts of gold, frankincense, and myrrh.*

12 *And having been warned by God in a dream not to return to Herod, the magi left for their own country by another way.*

DISCUSS with your GROUP or PONDER on your own . . .

Approximately when do these events take place?

Where do the magi find the Child?

How are the magi different from all the others who have heard the news about the Christ? In what ways does God lead them?

How do the magi respond to the star? How does this compare to Herod's response?

How do the magi respond to the dream?

Based on what you know of biblical history, why would people from the east be watching for the rise of a great King of the Jews?

INDUCTIVE FOCUS:

Questioning the Text

The key to exegesis (the fancy word meaning to draw meaning out of Scripture) is questioning the text. The basic investigative questions *Who? What? When? Where? Why?* and *How?* are your framework. Not every question can be addressed to every verse, and most verses require several variations on the same question. As we study God's Word together, realize that not every question that can be asked will be asked, but don't let that stop you from asking other questions and exploring further on your own. We will never run out of questions to ask and answers to glean from God's Word!

If you're at a loss for what questions to ask, pay attention to the words that you've marked. Go to your key words and start there with your questions! Marking not only helps you see the main idea, it always helps in asking questions.

Digging Deeper

The Magi and God's Witness to the Nations

If you have some extra time this week, see what you can discover about the magi. Start by carefully examining the text of Matthew, then read through the book of Daniel for a possible link to how men from the east knew of a coming Jewish Messiah.

Observations on Matthew:
What specifics does Matthew give us about the magi?

What commonly held "facts" about them aren't in Scripture?

Observations on Daniel:
What role did wise men play in eastern culture in Daniel's days?

What did the different nations Daniel served learn about the Hebrew God?

What had the nations been learning about the God of the Hebrews throughout His dealings in history? (Feel free to go beyond the book of Daniel on this one.)

SETTING the SCENE

Matthew 2 records back-to-back dreams. In these dreams God tells the magi to return home by way of another route and then Joseph, Mary, and Jesus to go to Egypt.

OBSERVE the TEXT of SCRIPTURE

READ Matthew 2:13-23 and **MARK** every occurrence of *dream*.

Matthew 2:13-23

13 Now when they had gone, behold, an angel of the Lord appeared to Joseph in a dream and said, "Get up! Take the Child and His mother and flee to Egypt, and remain there until I tell you; for Herod is going to search for the Child to destroy Him."

14 *So Joseph got up and took the Child and His mother while it was still night, and left for Egypt.*

15 *He remained there until the death of Herod. This was to fulfill what had been spoken by the Lord through the prophet: "OUT OF EGYPT I CALLED MY SON."*

16 *Then when Herod saw that he had been tricked by the magi, he became very enraged, and sent and slew all the male children who were in Bethlehem and all its vicinity, from two years old and under, according to the time which he had determined from the magi.*

17 *Then what had been spoken through Jeremiah the prophet was fulfilled:*

18 *"A VOICE WAS HEARD IN RAMAH,*

WEEPING AND GREAT MOURNING,

RACHEL WEEPING FOR HER CHILDREN;

AND SHE REFUSED TO BE COMFORTED,

BECAUSE THEY WERE NO MORE."

19 *But when Herod died, behold, an angel of the Lord appeared in a dream to Joseph in Egypt, and said,*

20 *"Get up, take the Child and His mother, and go into the land of Israel; for those who sought the Child's life are dead."*

21 *So Joseph got up, took the Child and His mother, and came into the land of Israel.*

22 *But when he heard that Archelaus was reigning over Judea in place of his father Herod, he was afraid to go there. Then after being warned by God in a dream, he left for the regions of Galilee,*

23 *and came and lived in a city called Nazareth. This was to fulfill what was spoken through the prophets: "He shall be called a Nazarene."*

DISCUSS with your GROUP or PONDER on your own . . .

How many significant dreams does God give Joseph according to this text? What does God specifically tell Joseph in these dreams?

How does Joseph respond?

How does Joseph's state of mind before his third dream compare with his state of mind before the first two he had?

Was Joseph's thinking "on track" before the third dream? What practical benefit did the third dream give him?

What prophecies does Matthew say are fulfilled in this series of events?

@THE END OF THE DAY . . .

Take some time to page back through the lesson and compare the different ways God spoke and the different people He spoke to. What commonalities did you see? What differences?

How did each of these people know they had encountered a Word from the Lord? How did each respond?

How are you doing at responding to the known Word of God in your life? Are you a Zacharias? A Mary? A magi? A Joseph? A Herod? And why?

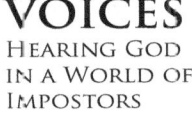

Week One: **Who Will You Listen To?**

WEEK TWO

Decreasing and Increasing

"He must increase, but I must decrease."
—John, the Baptist,
John 3:30

John the Baptist, the Messiah's much heralded herald, brings to a close the age of the prophets who pointed forward towards Jesus. The God who had spoken to the fathers in the prophets was about to speak clearly and definitively, no longer through an angel or a fallen human agent but through His very own Son. The game is about to change.

Week Two: **Decreasing and Increasing**

SETTING the SCENE

John's birth and work had been prophesied, but he began his ministry when the Word of God came to him.

OBSERVE the TEXT of SCRIPTURE

READ Luke 3:1-18 and **MARK** every reference to *John* including pronouns.

Luke 3:1-18

1 *Now in the fifteenth year of the reign of Tiberius Caesar, when Pontius Pilate was governor of Judea, and Herod was tetrarch of Galilee, and his brother Philip was tetrarch of the region of Ituraea and Trachonitis, and Lysanias was tetrarch of Abilene,*

2 *in the high priesthood of Annas and Caiaphas, the word of God came to John, the son of Zacharias, in the wilderness.*

3 *And he came into all the district around the Jordan, preaching a baptism of repentance for the forgiveness of sins;*

4 *as it is written in the book of the words of Isaiah the prophet,*

   "THE VOICE OF ONE CRYING IN THE WILDERNESS,

   'MAKE READY THE WAY OF THE LORD,

   MAKE HIS PATHS STRAIGHT.

5 *'EVERY RAVINE WILL BE FILLED,*

   AND EVERY MOUNTAIN AND HILL WILL BE BROUGHT LOW;

   THE CROOKED WILL BECOME STRAIGHT,

   AND THE ROUGH ROADS SMOOTH;

6 *AND ALL FLESH WILL SEE THE SALVATION OF GOD.' "*

7 *So he* began *saying to the crowds who were going out to be baptized by him,* "You brood of vipers, who warned you to flee from the wrath to come?

8 "Therefore bear fruits in keeping with repentance, and do not begin to say to yourselves, 'We have Abraham for our father,' for I say to you that from these stones God is able to raise up children to Abraham.

9 "Indeed the axe is already laid at the root of the trees; so every tree that does not bear good fruit is cut down and thrown into the fire."

10 *And the crowds were questioning him, saying,* "Then what shall we do?"

11 *And he* would answer and say to them, "The man who has two tunics is to share with him who has none; and he who has food is to do likewise."

12 *And some* tax collectors *also came to be baptized, and they said to him,* "Teacher, what shall we do?"

13 *And he said to them,* "Collect no more than what you have been ordered to."

14 Some *soldiers were questioning him, saying,* "And what about us, what shall we do?" *And he said to them,* "Do not take money from anyone by force, or accuse anyone *falsely, and be content with your wages."*

15 Now while the people were in a state of expectation and all were wondering in their hearts about John, as to whether he was the Christ,

16 John answered and said to them all, "As for me, I baptize you with water; but One is coming who is mightier than I, and I am not fit to untie the thong of His sandals; He will baptize you with the Holy Spirit and fire.

17 "His winnowing fork is in His hand to thoroughly clear His threshing floor, and to gather the wheat into His barn; but He will burn up the chaff with unquenchable fire."

18 So with many other exhortations he preached the gospel to the people.

DISCUSS with your GROUP or PONDER on your own . . .

When does the Word of God come to John? How precisely does Luke date this event? What regions and rulers does he mention?

How does John respond to the coming of the Word of God?

How quickly and thoroughly do you respond to the revealed Word of God and the promptings of the Holy Spirit?

How does John fulfill Isaiah's prophecy?

What do the people wonder about John?

Besides announcing Jesus' coming, what message from God does John proclaim? Has this message changed since then? How do you think the Church is doing at proclaiming it?

ONE STEP FURTHER:

Zacharias Prophecy

Luke informs us that John's father, Zacharias, is filled with the Holy Spirit and prophesies (1:67-80). This is significant because it is prior to the outpouring on believers at Pentecost.

If you have some extra time this week, check out what the Holy Spirit moves Zacharias to say about John and Jesus. Record your findings below.

VOICES
HEARING GOD
IN A WORLD OF
IMPOSTORS

SETTING the SCENE

Mark's Gospel gives the most succinct account of John the Baptist.

OBSERVE the TEXT of SCRIPTURE

READ Mark 1:1-11 and **MARK** every reference to *John*.

Mark 1:1-11

1 *The beginning of the gospel of Jesus Christ, the Son of God.*

2 *As it is written in Isaiah the prophet:*

"BEHOLD, I SEND MY MESSENGER AHEAD OF YOU,

WHO WILL PREPARE YOUR WAY;

3 *THE VOICE OF ONE CRYING IN THE WILDERNESS,*

'MAKE READY THE WAY OF THE LORD,

MAKE HIS PATHS STRAIGHT.' "

4 *John the Baptist appeared in the wilderness preaching a baptism of repentance for the forgiveness of sins.*

5 *And all the country of Judea was going out to him, and all the people of Jerusalem; and they were being baptized by him in the Jordan River, confessing their sins.*

6 *John was clothed with camel's hair and wore a leather belt around his waist, and his diet was locusts and wild honey.*

7 *And he was preaching, and saying, "After me One is coming who is mightier than I, and I am not fit to stoop down and untie the thong of His sandals.*

8 *"I baptized you with water; but He will baptize you with the Holy Spirit."*

9 *In those days Jesus came from Nazareth in Galilee and was baptized by John in the Jordan.*

10 *Immediately coming up out of the water, He saw the heavens opening, and the Spirit like a dove descending upon Him;*

11 *and a voice came out of the heavens: "You are My beloved Son, in You I am well-pleased."*

DISCUSS with your GROUP or PONDER on your own . . .

What two voices are mentioned in this text?

What is "the beginning of the gospel" message?

Who will precede the coming Lord? Where will he appear? What will he do? What will his message be?

Who is the first voice? Explain.

Where does the second voice come from? What does He say?

How does the second message confirm the first? Where else have we seen confirmation so far in the New Testament? In the Old Testament? What examples come to mind?

SETTING the SCENE

According to Matthew 4:12 Jesus withdrew into Galilee when He heard John had been taken into custody. The next mention of John the Baptist is in Matthew 11 when while still imprisoned he hears of Jesus' works.

OBSERVE the TEXT of SCRIPTURE

READ Matthew 11:2-6 and **UNDERLINE** every phrase describing the works of Christ.

Matthew 11:2-6

2 Now when John, while imprisoned, heard of the works of Christ, he sent word *by his disciples*

3 and said to Him, "Are You the Expected One, or shall we look for someone else?"

4 Jesus answered and said to them, "Go and report to John what you hear and see:

ONE STEP FURTHER:

John the Baptist Bio

John the Baptist is a hinge figure, the last of the great prophets to announce the Messiah's coming. There is a sense in which he truly has one foot in each age. If you have some extra time this week, compile a short outline or biography of the life and times of John the Baptist.

5 the *BLIND RECEIVE SIGHT* and the *lame walk, the lepers are cleansed and the deaf hear, the dead are raised up, and the POOR HAVE THE GOSPEL PREACHED TO THEM.*

6 *"And blessed is he who does not take offense at Me."*

DISCUSS with your GROUP or PONDER on your own . . .

Where is John?

What revelation has he had up to this point? What does he know and how does he know it? Cite your references, using a concordance if you need to.

Still, in spite of everything that has taken place, what question lingers in John's mind? How does Jesus answer him?

Now compare Jesus' answer in Matthew 11:5 with the following verses:

Matthew 11:5

". . . the *BLIND RECEIVE SIGHT* . . . the *deaf hear* . . . "

> **Isaiah 29:18**
>
> *On that day the deaf will hear words of a book,*
>
> *And out of their gloom and darkness the eyes of the blind will see.*

Matthew 11:5

". . . the *POOR HAVE THE GOSPEL PREACHED TO THEM.*"

> **Isaiah 61:1**
>
> *Because the LORD has anointed me*
>
> *To bring good news to the afflicted;*
>
> *He has sent me to bind up the brokenhearted,*
>
> *To proclaim liberty to captives*
>
> *And freedom to prisoners;*

Matthew 11:5

". . . the *dead are raised up* . . . "

> ### Isaiah 26:19
>
> *Your dead will live;*
>
> *Their corpses will rise.*
>
> *You who lie in the dust, awake and shout for joy,*
>
> *For your dew is as the dew of the dawn,*
>
> *And the earth will give birth to the departed spirits.*

How would you explain Jesus' answer? Where does He point John to? What can we learn from His approach.

INDUCTIVE FOCUS:

Scripture Interprets Scripture

While a good commentary is a student's friend, the best commentary on Scripture is Scripture itself. The more we read, the more we study, the more we see that Scripture interprets Scripture. To fully understand Isaiah, you need to hear what Jesus says about his prophecies. To fully understand the cross you need to understand the condition of man. Scripture itself is the best commentary!

Digging Deeper

More of the Gospels

If you have time this week, continue reading or listening to the Gospels. Luke and John are next on the docket. Again, as you read or listen, jot down the instances you note of God speaking to people and the contexts in which they happen.

Observations on Luke:

Observations on John:

VOICES
HEARING GOD
IN A WORLD OF
IMPOSTORS

New Testament

SETTING the SCENE

Having just eluded angry Jews trying to stone Him in Jerusalem, Jesus retreats to the area where John had been baptizing.

OBSERVE the TEXT of SCRIPTURE

READ John 10:40-42 and **MARK** distinctly references to *Jesus* and *John* including synonyms and pronouns.

John 10:40-42

40 *And He went away again beyond the Jordan to the place where John was first baptizing, and He was staying there.*

41 *Many came to Him and were saying, "While John performed no sign, yet everything John said about this man was true."*

42 *Many believed in Him there.*

DISCUSS with your GROUP or PONDER on your own . . .

Recalling the previous texts we've looked at, what had John testified about Jesus?

What did John's ministry involve? What *didn't* John do?

How did the people know he was the real deal?

How did John's work help people believe in Jesus?

Do your words and actions point people to Jesus? If so, how? If not, why not?

Digging Deeper

The Voice From Heaven at Jesus' Baptism

If you have some extra time this week, compare Jesus' baptism as it is recorded in each of the four Gospel accounts. Pay close attention to the voice from heaven and what it says. Note how John differs from the rest and how his record serves as an authentication for John the Baptist.

Matthew 3:13–17

Mark 1:9–11

Luke 3:21–23

John 1:29–33

MID-WAY RECAP . . .

Take a little time to scan back at all of the folks we've looked at so far and to compare what God spoke and how in each instance. Record what you've learned as well as any lingering questions.

WHAT DOES JESUS TEACH HIS FOLLOWERS?

Articles upon articles and books upon books have been written on hearing the voice of God. People over the ages have codified, systematized and laid out step by step how they thought it should be done and why. The question at hand today, though, is what does Jesus say in His Word? How did Jesus want His disciples then and now to live? We'll start by examining His teaching on prayer and then look at what He says about other things like signs, coming events, warnings, and false Christs.

PRAYER
SETTING the SCENE

Jesus teaches His disciples how to pray. The first text, Matthew 6:5-13, comes from the Sermon on the Mount, an extended teaching by Jesus recorded in Matthew 5–7. In the second text, Luke 11:1-13, Jesus teaches His disciples to pray in response to their request: "Lord, teach us to pray just as John also taught his disciples."

OBSERVE the TEXT of SCRIPTURE

READ Matthew 6:5-13 and **MARK** every occurrence of *pray*.

Matthew 6:5-13

5 *"When you pray, you are not to be like the hypocrites; for they love to stand and pray in the synagogues and on the street corners so that they may be seen by men. Truly I say to you, they have their reward in full.*

6 *"But you, when you pray, go into your inner room, close your door and pray to your Father who is in secret, and your Father who sees what is done in secret will reward you.*

7 *"And when you are praying, do not use meaningless repetition as the Gentiles do, for they suppose that they will be heard for their many words.*

8 *"So do not be like them; for your Father knows what you need before you ask Him.*

9 *"Pray, then, in this way:*

'Our Father who is in heaven,

Hallowed be Your name.

10 *'Your kingdom come.*

Your will be done,

On earth as it is in heaven.

11 *'Give us this day our daily bread.*

12 *'And forgive us our debts, as we also have forgiven our debtors.*

13 *'And do not lead us into temptation, but deliver us from evil. [For Yours is the kingdom and the power and the glory forever. Amen.]'*

DISCUSS with your GROUP or PONDER on your own . . .

What presuppositions do you have about prayer? Where did they come from?

ONE STEP FURTHER:

The Voices of Tradition

Jesus called out Jewish leaders on their habit of putting their traditions above the revealed Word of God. In Mark 7:8 He accuses the Pharisees and scribes: "Neglecting the commandment of God, you hold to the tradition of men."

Are there places in your life where you are relying on church tradition or some person's view as opposed to the clear and simple teaching of God's Word? Think and pray about it before you answer.

Who taught you how to pray? Where did the teaching originate?

What does Jesus tell the disciples not to do?

What does prayer to God presuppose according to verse 8?

After Jesus says "Pray then in this way," who does He mention first?

What are the disciples to pray with regard to God? What do these God-centered requests have to do with the disciples also?

What needs does Jesus tell His disciples to pray about in verses 11-13?

OBSERVE the TEXT of SCRIPTURE

READ Luke 11:1-13 and **MARK** every occurrence of *pray* and *ask*.

Luke 11:1-13

1   *It happened that while Jesus was praying in a certain place, after He had finished, one of His disciples said to Him, "Lord, teach us to pray just as John also taught his disciples."*

2   *And He said to them, "When you pray, say:*

    'Father, hallowed be Your name.

    Your kingdom come.

3   *'Give us each day our daily bread.*

ONE STEP FURTHER:

Jesus' Prayer Life

If you have some extra time this week, take a look at prayer in Jesus' life. How often did He pray? Where did He pray? How important was prayer in His day-to-day existence on earth? Record your findings below and consider what you can learn from Jesus' example to apply in your life.

4 *'And forgive us our sins,*

For we ourselves also forgive everyone who is indebted to us.

And lead us not into temptation.' "

5 *Then He said to them, "Suppose one of you has a friend, and goes to him at midnight and says to him, 'Friend, lend me three loaves;*

6 *for a friend of mine has come to me from a journey, and I have nothing to set before him';*

7 *and from inside he answers and says, 'Do not bother me; the door has already been shut and my children and I are in bed; I cannot get up and give you anything.'*

8 *"I tell you, even though he will not get up and give him anything because he is his friend, yet because of his persistence he will get up and give him as much as he needs.*

9 *"So I say to you, ask, and it will be given to you; seek, and you will find; knock, and it will be opened to you.*

10 *"For everyone who asks, receives; and he who seeks, finds; and to him who knocks, it will be opened.*

11 *"Now suppose one of you fathers is asked by his son for a fish; he will not give him a snake instead of a fish, will he?*

12 *"Or if he is asked for an egg, he will not give him a scorpion, will he?*

13 *"If you then, being evil, know how to give good gifts to your children, how much more will your heavenly Father give the Holy Spirit to those who ask Him?"*

DISCUSS with your GROUP or PONDER on your own . . .

What prompts the disciples to ask Jesus to teach them to pray?

What does He tell them? How does this compare with His teaching according to Matthew?

What two illustrations does Jesus use to encourage them that their Father will give them what they need?

Based on the story of the friend at midnight, what does Jesus tell His disciples to do? Why?

Does He give specifics on how people will receive, find, and have doors opened? What assurance does He give?

What lesson does Jesus teach from the example of the father who gives good gifts?

What good gift does Jesus say the Father will give? According to John 16:13-14 what does the Spirit do for us?

So, can we expect answers from God? Do we know exactly what they'll be? Explain

FYI:

Parallel Account from the Sermon on the Mount

"Ask, and it will be given to you; seek, and you will find; knock, and it will be opened to you. For everyone who asks receives, and he who seeks finds, and to him who knocks it will be opened. Or what man is there among you who, when his son asks for a loaf, will give him a stone?

Or if he asks for a fish, he will not give him a snake, will he? If you then, being evil, know how to give good gifts to your children, how much more will your Father who is in heaven give what is good to those who ask Him!

In everything, therefore, treat people the same way you want them to treat you, for this is the Law and the Prophets."

—Jesus, Matthew 7:7-12

Digging Deeper

Quoting Scripture Doesn't Make You Orthodox

Turns out even Satan quotes Scripture. If you have some extra time this week, examine Satan's use of Scripture in the temptation accounts. What scriptures does he use? How does he try to tempt Jesus with them? How "orthodox" does he sound? How does Jesus respond?

Matthew 4:1-11

Luke 4:1-13

My biggest takeaway from examining and comparing these accounts . . .

VOICES

HEARING GOD
IN A WORLD OF
IMPOSTORS

New Testament

ONE STEP FURTHER:

Word Study: Signs

If you're ever going to do a word study, do this one: find the Greek word for "sign" and see how it is used in the New Testament. Specifically, look at its use in the following categories:

The Gospels (Matthew, Mark, Luke, and John—recording the life and times of Jesus.)

Acts (The beginning of the Church age and the lives of the Apostles.)

The Letters (Romans through Jude—letters to first century Churches and individuals concerning doctrine and life in Christ.)

Revelation (The revelation of Jesus Christ about "the things which must soon take place.")

Where does the word appear most often? Where is it used least often? Under what circumstances is it a positive word? When is it negative? Record your observations, additional thoughts, and questions below.

SIGNS
SETTING the SCENE

There is no question that the Old Testament Scriptures predicted that the coming Messiah would perform signs: the blind would receive sight, the lame walk, the deaf hear, the dead be raised. Scripture tells us that Jesus often healed people to show His authority to forgive sin. Signs and wonders also authenticated the Gospel as it went forth to the Gentiles. What, though, does Jesus say about sign and wonder *seekers*? Let's look for ourselves.

OBSERVE the TEXT of SCRIPTURE

READ Matthew 12:38-40 and **MARK** every occurrence of *sign*.

Matthew 12:38-40

38 Then some of the scribes and Pharisees said to Him, "Teacher, we want to see a sign from You."

39 But He answered and said to them, "An evil and adulterous generation craves for a sign; and yet no sign will be given to it but the sign of Jonah the prophet;

40 for just as JONAH WAS THREE DAYS AND THREE NIGHTS IN THE BELLY OF THE SEA MONSTER, so will the Son of Man be three days and three nights in the heart of the earth.

DISCUSS with your GROUP or PONDER on your own . . .

Who asks Jesus for a sign? How does He respond? How does He characterize those who crave signs? What is the only sign He says He will give them?

What is the context in which they ask? Has Jesus been hiding in a corner? (If you need to, go back and read the rest of Matthew 12.)

Do we resemble this sign-seeking generation? If so, what does that say about us? Explain.

SETTING the SCENE

Jesus is the speaker in this section from Luke's Gospel account.

OBSERVE the TEXT of SCRIPTURE

READ Luke 16:19-31 and **MARK** the phrase *Moses and the Prophets*, including pronouns.

Luke 16:19-31

19 "Now there was a rich man, and he habitually dressed in purple and fine linen, joyously living in splendor every day.

20 "And a poor man named Lazarus was laid at his gate, covered with sores,

21 and longing to be fed with the crumbs which were falling from the rich man's table; besides, even the dogs were coming and licking his sores.

22 "Now the poor man died and was carried away by the angels to Abraham's bosom; and the rich man also died and was buried.

23 "In Hades he lifted up his eyes, being in torment, and saw Abraham far away and Lazarus in his bosom.

24 "And he cried out and said, 'Father Abraham, have mercy on me, and send Lazarus so that he may dip the tip of his finger in water and cool off my tongue, for I am in agony in this flame.'

25 "But Abraham said, 'Child, remember that during your life you received your good things, and likewise Lazarus bad things; but now he is being comforted here, and you are in agony.

26 'And besides all this, between us and you there is a great chasm fixed, so that those who wish to come over from here to you will not be able, and that none may cross over from there to us.'

27 "And he said, 'Then I beg you, father, that you send him to my father's house—

28 for I have five brothers—in order that he may warn them, so that they will not also come to this place of torment.'

29 "But Abraham said, 'They have Moses and the Prophets; let them hear them.'

30 "But he said, 'No, father Abraham, but if someone goes to them from the dead, they will repent!'

31 "But he said to him, 'If they do not listen to Moses and the Prophets, they will not be persuaded even if someone rises from the dead.' "

FYI:

Different Cravings

While "an evil and adulterous generation craves [Greek: *epizeteo*] for a sign" (Matthew 12:39), the heroes of the faith recorded in Hebrews 11 were "seeking [Greek: *epizeteo*] a country of their own," the better, heavenly country God has prepared for them (Hebrews 11:14-16)—same Greek word, far different objects and outcomes. What do you crave? What are you seeking today?

DISCUSS with your GROUP or PONDER on your own . . .

Briefly describe the scene.

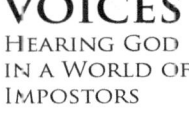

VOICES

HEARING GOD
IN A WORLD OF
IMPOSTORS

What does the rich man ask for on behalf of his brothers? Why?

According to Abraham, what sufficient revelation do the brothers have? What will they also reject if they reject this revelation?

Can signs alone make a person believe? Support your answer from Scripture.

SETTING the SCENE

After scoffing at his fellow disciples' witness to the risen Christ, doubting Thomas finally believes.

OBSERVE the TEXT of SCRIPTURE

READ John 20:24-29 and **MARK** every reference to *seeing*. Also **MARK** every occurrence of *believe*.

John 20:24-29

24 But Thomas, one of the twelve, called Didymus, was not with them when Jesus came.

25 So the other disciples were saying to him, "We have seen the Lord!" But he said to them, "Unless I see in His hands the imprint of the nails, and put my finger into the place of the nails, and put my hand into His side, I will not believe."

26 After eight days His disciples were again inside, and Thomas with them. Jesus came, the doors having been shut, and stood in their midst and said, "Peace be with you."

27 Then He said to Thomas, "Reach here with your finger, and see My hands; and reach here your hand and put it into My side; and do not be unbelieving, but believing."

28 Thomas answered and said to Him, "My Lord and my God!"

29 Jesus said to him, "Because you have seen Me, have you believed? Blessed are they who did not see, and yet believed."

DISCUSS with your GROUP or PONDER on your own . . .

What have the other disciples seen for themselves?

Why did Thomas continue to doubt after hearing their witness?

What did Thomas need to overcome his unbelief? Does Jesus give this to him?

Who does Jesus called "blessed" in verse 29?

Can it be said of you today that you "did not see, and yet believed"?

@THE END OF THE DAY . . .

As we finish off our time for the week, page back through the lesson and summarize your key takeaway points. Here are a few questions to help you think this through:

• What truth did you already know that has been confirmed?

• Did you learn something new? If so, what was it?

• Have any of your views shifted to be more in line with the revealed Word of God? If so, what?

My key takeaway point from this week is . . .

FYI:

Why John Records the Signs

Therefore many other signs Jesus also performed in the presence of the disciples, which are not written in this book; but these have been written so that you may believe that Jesus is the Christ, the Son of God; and that believing you may have life in His name.

—John 20:30-31

VOICES
HEARING GOD
IN A WORLD OF
IMPOSTORS

WEEK THREE

Keep Watching

"Be on the alert then, for you do not know the day nor the hour."
—Jesus,
Matthew 25:13

Jesus performed signs, there's no arguing that one. So that people would know He had authority to forgive sins, He healed bodies. As fulfillment of prophecy He caused the blind to see, the deaf to hear, and the dead to rise. Oh yeah, Jesus performed signs while He walked the earth, but He affirmed faith. This week we're going to look more closely at His life and ministry and at the clear commands He gives His disciples about living in the time between His first and second comings.

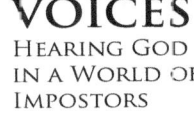

Peter's Confession and Rejection

Simon Peter answered, "You are the Christ, the Son of the living God."

And Jesus said to him, "Blessed are you, Simon Barjona, because flesh and blood did not reveal this to you, but My Father who is in heaven."

—Matthew 16:16-17

This same Peter who declares Jesus to be the Christ, will not think clearly when Jesus reveals more truth—truth he won't like: about a kingdom that is not of this world.

ONE STEP FURTHER:

Take Up Your Cross

Take some time this week to measure modern teachings you've heard against what Jesus taught plainly: "If anyone wishes to come after Me, he must deny himself, and take up his cross and follow Me." How do voices you've heard measure up against this plain biblical truth?

Week Three: **Keep Watching**

THINK IN ACCORDANCE WITH THE WORD

Jesus expected His followers to think. Paul will emphasize the renewed mind in his letters, but even prior to the coming of the Holy Spirit, Jesus points to the importance of clear thinking.

SETTING the SCENE

Peter has just confessed Jesus to be the Christ. His facts are straight and his thinking seems to be clear.

OBSERVE the TEXT of SCRIPTURE

READ Mark 8:31-38. **MARK** every reference to *Peter*, including pronouns. **UNDERLINE** every phrase that describes being a disciple.

Mark 8:31-38

31 *And He began to teach them that the Son of Man must suffer many things and be rejected by the elders and the chief priests and the scribes, and be killed, and after three days rise again.*

32 *And He was stating the matter plainly. And Peter took Him aside and began to rebuke Him.*

33 *But turning around and seeing His disciples, He rebuked Peter and said, "Get behind Me, Satan; for you are not setting your mind on God's interests, but man's."*

34 *And He summoned the crowd with His disciples, and said to them, "If anyone wishes to come after Me, he must deny himself, and take up his cross and follow Me.*

35 *"For whoever wishes to save his life will lose it, but whoever loses his life for My sake and the gospel's will save it.*

36 *"For what does it profit a man to gain the whole world, and forfeit his soul?*

37 *"For what will a man give in exchange for his soul?*

38 *"For whoever is ashamed of Me and My words in this adulterous and sinful generation, the Son of Man will also be ashamed of him when He comes in the glory of His Father with the holy angels."*

DISCUSS with your GROUP or PONDER on your own . . .

What does Jesus teach the disciples in verse 31? According to verse 32 how does He say it?

What does Peter do in response to Jesus' teaching?

Do you ever actively oppose truth? Explain.

How does Jesus describe Peter's thinking? Remembering the context, what makes this so remarkable?

What are some ways we set our minds on man's interests and dress them up as God's will?

How does Jesus illustrate a life set on God's mind and will?

What are followers not to be ashamed of?

Where do we know we have His Words?

Where did Peter drop the ball? Do you ever drop the ball with reference to the revealed words of Christ? Explain.

ONE STEP FURTHER:

Hearts of Stones and Hearts of Flesh

Before we throw Peter under the bus as a complete knucklehead, let's remember that he lived prior to the coming of the Holy Spirit. Sure he palled around with Jesus, but the Spirit did not indwell him until Pentecost. The New Covenant had not yet been cut whereby Peter's heart of stone would be replaced with a heart of flesh. If you have a chance this week, check out Jeremiah's prophecy about new hearts and a new covenant in Jeremiah 31:33-34. Then record your observations below.

VOICES
HEARING GOD
IN A WORLD OF
IMPOSTORS

SETTING the SCENE

According to the next text, Mary and Joseph lose track of Jesus on a trip to Jerusalem. Talk about a hard teaching moment for the grown-ups!

OBSERVE the TEXT of SCRIPTURE

READ Luke 2:41-52 and **MARK** every reference to *Jesus*.

Luke 2:41-52

41 *Now His parents went to Jerusalem every year at the Feast of the Passover.*

42 *And when He became twelve, they went up there according to the custom of the Feast;*

43 *and as they were returning, after spending the full number of days, the boy Jesus stayed behind in Jerusalem. But His parents were unaware of it,*

44 *but supposed Him to be in the caravan, and went a day's journey; and they began looking for Him among their relatives and acquaintances.*

45 *When they did not find Him, they returned to Jerusalem looking for Him.*

46 *Then, after three days they found Him in the temple, sitting in the midst of the teachers, both listening to them and asking them questions.*

47 *And all who heard Him were amazed at His understanding and His answers.*

48 *When they saw Him, they were astonished; and His mother said to Him, "Son, why have You treated us this way? Behold, Your father and I have been anxiously looking for You."*

49 *And He said to them, "Why is it that you were looking for Me? Did you not know that I had to be in My Father's house?"*

50 *But they did not understand the statement which He had made to them.*

51 *And He went down with them and came to Nazareth, and He continued in subjection to them; and His mother treasured all these things in her heart.*

52 *And Jesus kept increasing in wisdom and stature, and in favor with God and men.*

DISCUSS with your GROUP or PONDER on your own . . .

Why were Jesus and His family in Jerusalem? Why does Jesus stay there?

How long does it take for Mary and Joseph to realize He is missing? Where do they finally find Him? What is He doing?

How does Jesus respond to His anxious mother? According to Him, what should she and Joseph have known? Why should they have known it?

Are there things we should know that we continue to seek guidance for simply because we're not giving full attention to the revelation we already have? What types of things? What specific things?

Digging Deeper

Have you not read?

Researchers tell us that the New Testament writers make 224 direct references to the Old Testament and cite allusions to Old Testament scriptures anywhere from 600 to 1,600 times. In round numbers about 10% of the New Testament either quotes the Old directly or makes clear allusion to it. This week, if you have some time, examine Jesus' view of the Old Testament.*

How often and under what conditions does Jesus say "It is written . . . ."?

How else does Jesus refer to the Old Testament and use it in His teaching?

What is Jesus' view of the Old Testament? Cite specific examples.

Why does this matter?

*http://www.bible-researcher.com/nicole.html (The following essay by Roger Nicole is reproduced from *Revelation and the Bible*, ed. by Carl. F.H. Henry. Grand Rapids: Baker, 1958, pp. 137-151.)

WHAT NOT TO DO . . .

SETTING the SCENE

In an account recorded in each of the synoptic Gospels—Mark 13, Matthew 24, and Luke 21—Jesus warns His disciples about the days to come. This passage is often referred to as the Olivet Discourse.

OBSERVE the TEXT of SCRIPTURE

READ Mark 13 and **UNDERLINE** every instruction and warning Jesus gives.

Mark 13

1 As He was going out of the temple, one of His disciples said to Him, "Teacher, behold what wonderful stones and what wonderful buildings!"

2 And Jesus said to him, "Do you see these great buildings? Not one stone will be left upon another which will not be torn down."

3 As He was sitting on the Mount of Olives opposite the temple, Peter and James and John and Andrew were questioning Him privately,

4 "Tell us, when will these things be, and what will be the sign when all these things are going to be fulfilled?"

5 And Jesus began to say to them, "See to it that no one misleads you.

6 "Many will come in My name, saying, 'I am He!' and will mislead many.

7 "When you hear of wars and rumors of wars, do not be frightened; those things must take place; but that is not yet the end.

8 "For nation will rise up against nation, and kingdom against kingdom; there will be earthquakes in various places; there will also be famines. These things are merely the beginning of birth pangs.

9 "But be on your guard; for they will deliver you to the courts, and you will be flogged in the synagogues, and you will stand before governors and kings for My sake, as a testimony to them.

10 "The gospel must first be preached to all the nations.

11 "When they arrest you and hand you over, do not worry beforehand about what you are to say, but say whatever is given you in that hour; for it is not you who speak, but it is the Holy Spirit.

12 "Brother will betray brother to death, and a father his child; and children will rise up against parents and have them put to death.

13 "You will be hated by all because of My name, but the one who endures to the end, he will be saved.

14 "But when you see the ABOMINATION OF DESOLATION standing where it should not be (let the reader understand), then those who are in Judea must flee to the mountains.

15 "The one who is on the housetop must not go down, or go in to get anything out of his house;

16 and the one who is in the field must not turn back to get his coat.

17 "But woe to those who are pregnant and to those who are nursing babies in those days!

18 "But pray that it may not happen in the winter.

19 "For those days will be a time of tribulation such as has not occurred since the beginning of the creation which God created until now, and never will.

20 "Unless the Lord had shortened those days, no life would have been saved; but for the sake of the elect, whom He chose, He shortened the days.

21 "And then if anyone says to you, 'Behold, here is the Christ'; or, 'Behold, He is there'; do not believe him;

22 for false Christs and false prophets will arise, and will show signs and wonders, in order to lead astray, if possible, the elect.

23 "But take heed; behold, I have told you everything in advance.

24 "But in those days, after that tribulation, THE SUN WILL BE DARKENED AND THE MOON WILL NOT GIVE ITS LIGHT,

25 AND THE STARS WILL BE FALLING from heaven, and the powers that are in the heavens will be shaken.

26 "Then they will see THE SON OF MAN COMING IN CLOUDS with great power and glory.

27 "And then He will send forth the angels, and will gather together His elect from the four winds, from the farthest end of the earth to the farthest end of heaven.

28 "Now learn the parable from the fig tree: when its branch has already become tender and puts forth its leaves, you know that summer is near.

29 "Even so, you too, when you see these things happening, recognize that He is near, right at the door.

30 "Truly I say to you, this generation will not pass away until all these things take place.

31 "Heaven and earth will pass away, but My words will not pass away.

32 "But of that day or hour no one knows, not even the angels in heaven, nor the Son, but the Father alone.

33 "Take heed, keep on the alert; for you do not know when the appointed time will come.

34 "It is like a man away on a journey, who upon leaving his house and putting his slaves in charge, assigning to each one his task, also commanded the doorkeeper to stay on the alert.

35 "Therefore, be on the alert—for you do not know when the master of the house is coming, whether in the evening, at midnight, or when the rooster crows, or in the morning—

36 in case he should come suddenly and find you asleep.

37 "What I say to you I say to all, 'Be on the alert!' "

ONE STEP FURTHER:

Will Not Pass Away

If you have some extra time this week, think through what Scripture says about the permanence of the Word of God. Use your concordance if you need to. Some search terms that may help are 'pass away" and "forever." Record what you find below.

VOICES
HEARING GOD
IN A WORLD OF
IMPOSTORS

Week Three: **Keep Watching**

DISCUSS with your GROUP or PONDER on your own . . .

Where does this conversation take place? Who is Jesus talking to?

What do the disciples ask Jesus in verse 4 and how does He respond? Are His first words an answer or something else? Explain.

What first danger does He warn about? How pervasive will it be?

How diligent are they to be in the face of coming threats?

In verse 7, what else does Jesus instruct His follows "not to be"? Why? What are they to do instead?

What does Jesus say about the Holy Spirit in verse 11? What are the circumstances and what is the purpose?

Describe the trajectory of these days. [Be on guard as to how this differs from a lot of "churchy" teaching.]

What are Jesus' specific warnings in verses 21-23?

Humans

What will the message be? What will accompany the message? What will the purpose be?

Based on the whole passage, what kind of signs are Christians instructed to watch for?

What does Jesus say will pass away? What won't pass away? If false Christs and prophets are coming (and they are) what is our ultimate plumbline to be?

What does Jesus tell us to do in the face of these impending times? What will this involve?

How can you be on alert today?

WHAT TO DO . . .

SETTING the SCENE

Jesus tells a parable about how to live when the Master is away.

OBSERVE the TEXT of SCRIPTURE

READ Matthew 25:1-13 and **MARK** every reference to the wise virgins.

Matthew 25:1-13

1   *"Then the kingdom of heaven will be comparable to ten virgins, who took their lamps and went out to meet the bridegroom.*

2   *"Five of them were foolish, and five were prudent.*

3   *"For when the foolish took their lamps, they took no oil with them,*

VOICES
HEARING GOD
IN A WORLD OF
IMPOSTORS

New Testament

4   *but the prudent took oil in flasks along with their lamps.*

5   *"Now while the bridegroom was delaying, they all got drowsy and began to sleep.*

6   *"But at midnight there was a shout, 'Behold, the bridegroom! Come out to meet him.'*

7   *"Then all those virgins rose and trimmed their lamps.*

8   *"The foolish said to the prudent, 'Give us some of your oil, for our lamps are going out.'*

9   *"But the prudent answered, 'No, there will not be enough for us and you too; go instead to the dealers and buy some for yourselves.'*

10 *"And while they were going away to make the purchase, the bridegroom came, and those who were ready went in with him to the wedding feast; and the door was shut.*

11 *"Later the other virgins also came, saying, 'Lord, lord, open up for us.'*

12 *"But he answered, 'Truly I say to you, I do not know you.'*

13 *"Be on the alert then, for you do not know the day nor the hour.*

DISCUSS with your GROUP or PONDER on your own . . .

Who are the main characters in this account?

What distinguishes the wise virgins from the foolish ones?

What happens when the foolish virgins go to buy more oil?

What is Jesus teaching His disciples then and now? How can you live "on the alert"?

READ Matthew 25:14-30 and **MARK** every reference to the *master.*

Matthew 25:14-30

14 *"For it is just like a man about to go on a journey, who called his own slaves and entrusted his possessions to them.*

15 *"To one he gave five talents, to another, two, and to another, one, each according to his own ability; and he went on his journey.*

16 *"Immediately the one who had received the five talents went and traded with them, and gained five more talents.*

17 *"In the same manner the one who had received the two talents gained two more.*

18 *"But he who received the one talent went away, and dug a hole in the ground and hid his master's money.*

19 *"Now after a long time the master of those slaves came and settled accounts with them.*

20 *"The one who had received the five talents came up and brought five more talents, saying, 'Master, you entrusted five talents to me. See, I have gained five more talents.'*

21 *"His master said to him, 'Well done, good and faithful slave. You were faithful with a few things, I will put you in charge of many things; enter into the joy of your master.'*

22 *"Also the one who had received the two talents came up and said, 'Master, you entrusted two talents to me. See, I have gained two more talents.'*

23 *"His master said to him, 'Well done, good and faithful slave. You were faithful with a few things, I will put you in charge of many things; enter into the joy of your master.'*

24 *"And the one also who had received the one talent came up and said, 'Master, I knew you to be a hard man, reaping where you did not sow and gathering where you scattered no seed.*

25 *'And I was afraid, and went away and hid your talent in the ground. See, you have what is yours.'*

26 *"But his master answered and said to him, 'You wicked, lazy slave, you knew that I reap where I did not sow and gather where I scattered no seed.*

27 *'Then you ought to have put my money in the bank, and on my arrival I would have received my money back with interest.*

28 *'Therefore take away the talent from him, and give it to the one who has the ten talents.'*

29 *"For to everyone who has, more shall be given, and he will have an abundance; but from the one who does not have, even what he does have shall be taken away.*

30 *"Throw out the worthless slave into the outer darkness; in that place there will be weeping and gnashing of teeth.*

FYI:

The Wicked Slave
Although the slave given one talent claimed he buried the money because he knew his master—"I knew you to be a hard man"—in truth he did not know the master fully and he did not know the master's heart. He was the only one of the three servants who was thrown out. Truly knowing the Master makes all the difference.

VOICES
HEARING GOD
IN A WORLD OF
IMPOSTORS

Week Three: **Keep Watching**

DISCUSS with your GROUP or PONDER on your own . . .

How does this parable compare with the parable of the ten virgins?

Why does this man entrust money to his slaves? Where does he go? For how long?

What does the master of the slaves expect to happen in his absence?

Which slaves meet his expectations? How does the master describe them? What do they do and what do they receive?

Which slave does not meet expectations? What is his view of the master and how he works? What is his excuse?

ONE STEP FURTHER:

Your Stewardship
Take some time this week to consider what you're doing with the stewardship entrusted to you. How does your view of your Master impact how you're living? Does knowing your Master free you to live without fear while He is "away"?

How does the master describe him? What happens to him?

What talents are you holding in your hand today?

What is your view of God and how He works.?

Are you living faithfully or fearfully? Does anything need reacjusting? Explain.

@THE END OF THE DAY . . .

Next week we'll continue listening to Jesus in the Gospels, specifically focusing on His Words to His disciples before departing from them to return to the Father. For now, take some time to review and process what you've learned this week then jot down what you need to remember in the space below. Remember, sometimes less is more.

Week Three: **Keep Watching**

Week Four

Words in the Upper Room

"These things I have spoken to you while abiding with you. But the Helper, the Holy Spirit, whom the Father will send in My name, He will teach you all things, and bring to your remembrance all that I said to you."
—Jesus
John 14:25-26

Before He goes to the cross, Jesus instructs His disciples in a passage often referred to as the Upper Room Discourse. It's found in John 14–17. This is a critical text on how to live in the post-cross world. As we study this week, more than anything else read the text, re-read the text, and read it some more. When you're done, read it again.

HOW TO LIVE WHEN JESUS GOES TO THE FATHER

OBSERVE the TEXT of SCRIPTURE

READ John 14. **IDENTIFY** and **MARK** key repeating words that you notice. Make sure to include the *Spirit of truth*, along with synonyms and pronouns.

John 14

1   "Do not let your heart be troubled; believe in God, believe also in Me.

2   "In My Father's house are many dwelling places; if it were not so, I would have told you; for I go to prepare a place for you.

3   "If I go and prepare a place for you, I will come again and receive you to Myself, that where I am, there you may be also.

4   "And you know the way where I am going."

5   Thomas said to Him, "Lord, we do not know where You are going, how do we know the way?"

6   Jesus said to him, "I am the way, and the truth, and the life; no one comes to the Father but through Me.

7   "If you had known Me, you would have known My Father also; from now on you know Him, and have seen Him."

8   Philip said to Him, "Lord, show us the Father, and it is enough for us."

9   Jesus said to him, "Have I been so long with you, and yet you have not come to know Me, Philip? He who has seen Me has seen the Father; how can you say, 'Show us the Father'?

10 "Do you not believe that I am in the Father, and the Father is in Me? The words that I say to you I do not speak on My own initiative, but the Father abiding in Me does His works.

11 "Believe Me that I am in the Father and the Father is in Me; otherwise believe because of the works themselves.

12 "Truly, truly, I say to you, he who believes in Me, the works that I do, he will do also; and greater works than these he will do; because I go to the Father.

13 "Whatever you ask in My name, that will I do, so that the Father may be glorified in the Son.

14 "If you ask Me anything in My name, I will do it.

15 "If you love Me, you will keep My commandments.

16 "I will ask the Father, and He will give you another Helper, that He may be with you forever;

17 that is the Spirit of truth, whom the world cannot receive, because it does not see Him or know Him, but you know Him because He abides with you and will be in you.

18 "I will not leave you as orphans; I will come to you.

19 "After a little while the world will no longer see Me, but you will see Me; because I live, you will live also.

20 "In that day you will know that I am in My Father, and you in Me, and I in you.

ONE STEP FURTHER:

"In My Name"

What does asking in Jesus' name mean? Is it more than a phrase to tack on to the end of a prayer? If you have some extra time this week, use your concordance and other study tools to see what you can discover about John's usage of this phrase, as well as how it is used elsewhere in Scripture. Record your findings below.

ONE STEP FURTHER:

Word Study: Believe

If you have some extra time this week see what you can find out about the Greek words *pistis* (faith) and *pisteuo* (believe). How does John use them? How do other New Testament writers use them? How would you answer the question: *What does it mean to believe in Jesus?*

21 "He who has My commandments and keeps them is the one who loves Me; and he who loves Me will be loved by My Father, and I will love him and will disclose Myself to him."

22 Judas (not Iscariot) said to Him, "Lord, what then has happened that You are going to disclose Yourself to us and not to the world?"

23 Jesus answered and said to him, "If anyone loves Me, he will keep My word; and My Father will love him, and We will come to him and make Our abode with him.

24 "He who does not love Me does not keep My words; and the word which you hear is not Mine, but the Father's who sent Me.

25 "These things I have spoken to you while abiding with you.

26 "But the Helper, the Holy Spirit, whom the Father will send in My name, He will teach you all things, and bring to your remembrance all that I said to you.

27 "Peace I leave with you; My peace I give to you; not as the world gives do I give to you. Do not let your heart be troubled, nor let it be fearful.

28 "You heard that I said to you, 'I go away, and I will come to you.' If you loved Me, you would have rejoiced because I go to the Father, for the Father is greater than I.

29 "Now I have told you before it happens, so that when it happens you may believe.

30 "I will not speak much more with you, for the ruler of the world is coming, and he has nothing in Me;

31 but so that the world may know that I love the Father, I do exactly as the Father commanded Me. Get up, let us go from here.

DISCUSS with your GROUP or PONDER on your own . . .

Overview the Text

Describe the setting. Who is Jesus talking to? What topics does He address?

What repeating words did you notice?

John 14:1-15 Questions

What does Jesus command His disciples?

FYI:

When Grammar Matters
The way we can distinguish a command from a simple statement is by the grammatical mood. "The indicative mood merely states. The imperative mood commands.

ONE STEP FURTHER:

Identifying Imperatives
If you have some extra time this week, see if you can identify instances of the imperative mood in John 14. Record your findings below.

Week Four: **Words in the Upper Room**

What does He promise?

What general statements does He make? About the disciples? About Himself?

What does knowing the Father have to do with knowing Jesus? According to verse 10, why and how does Jesus speak and work?

What does Jesus say about asking in His name?

What conditional ("if") statements does Jesus make in this section? How do they apply to Jesus? To His disciples?

According to John 14:15, how do we know if we love Jesus? What are His commandments?

John 14:16-18 Questions

List everything you learn about the Helper in verses 16-18.

What kind of relationship will disciples have with the Holy Spirit? How long will it last?

John 14:19-30 Questions

What day is Jesus referring to in verse 20? Explain. What will Jesus' disciples know?

Describe the person who loves Jesus according to verses 21 and 23. What is involved in this? What benefit will result? What is the corresponding truth in verse 24?

Can we separate the Father's words from Jesus' words? Why/why not? Explain.

When did Jesus do His speaking according to verse 25? What tense is the verb "have spoken"?

How will the Holy Spirit continue to help believers? How His ministry relate to Jesus' ministry and words?

How can the world know that Jesus loves the Father? Does this relate to how the world will know His disciples love Him? Explain.

What commandment does Jesus repeat and then expand upon in verse 27?

Why can the disciples have peace? Why should they be rejoicing?

Is your love for Jesus a biblical love? Explain.

VOICES
HEARING GOD
IN A WORLD OF
IMPOSTORS

Week Four: **Words in the Upper Room**

How can the truth of this passage empower us to live with untroubled hearts?

What difference does the indwelling Holy Spirit make in your life today? What does the Word say we're like without Him?

OBSERVE the TEXT of SCRIPTURE

READ John 15. **IDENTIFY** and **MARK** key repeating words. Make sure to **MARK** *abide* and in a distinct fashion **MARK** the two kinds of *branches*.

John 15

1 *"I am the true vine, and My Father is the vinedresser.*

2 *"Every branch in Me that does not bear fruit, He takes away; and every branch that bears fruit, He prunes it so that it may bear more fruit.*

3 *"You are already clean because of the word which I have spoken to you.*

4 *"Abide in Me, and I in you. As the branch cannot bear fruit of itself unless it abides in the vine, so neither can you unless you abide in Me.*

5 *"I am the vine, you are the branches; he who abides in Me and I in him, he bears much fruit, for apart from Me you can do nothing.*

6 *"If anyone does not abide in Me, he is thrown away as a branch and dries up; and they gather them, and cast them into the fire and they are burned.*

7 *"If you abide in Me, and My words abide in you, ask whatever you wish, and it will be done for you.*

8 *"My Father is glorified by this, that you bear much fruit, and so prove to be My disciples.*

9 *"Just as the Father has loved Me, I have also loved you; abide in My love.*

10 *"If you keep My commandments, you will abide in My love; just as I have kept My Father's commandments and abide in His love.*

11 *"These things I have spoken to you so that My joy may be in you, and that your joy may be made full.*

12 *"This is My commandment, that you love one another, just as I have loved you.*

13 *"Greater love has no one than this, that one lay down his life for his friends.*

14 *"You are My friends if you do what I command you.*

15 *"No longer do I call you slaves, for the slave does not know what his master is doing; but I have called you friends, for all things that I have heard from My Father I have made known to you.*

HEARING GOD IN A WORLD OF IMPOSTORS

New Testament

16 *"You did not choose Me but I chose you, and appointed you that you would go and bear fruit, and that your fruit would remain, so that whatever you ask of the Father in My name He may give to you.*

17 *"This I command you, that you love one another.*

18 *"If the world hates you, you know that it has hated Me before it hated you.*

19 *"If you were of the world, the world would love its own; but because you are not of the world, but I chose you out of the world, because of this the world hates you.*

20 *"Remember the word that I said to you, 'A slave is not greater than his master.' If they persecuted Me, they will also persecute you; if they kept My word, they will keep yours also.*

21 *"But all these things they will do to you for My name's sake, because they do not know the One who sent Me.*

22 *"If I had not come and spoken to them, they would not have sin, but now they have no excuse for their sin.*

23 *"He who hates Me hates My Father also.*

24 *"If I had not done among them the works which no one else did, they would not have sin; but now they have both seen and hated Me and My Father as well.*

25 *"But they have done this to fulfill the word that is written in their Law, 'THEY HATED ME WITHOUT A CAUSE.'*

26 *"When the Helper comes, whom I will send to you from the Father, that is the Spirit of truth who proceeds from the Father, He will testify about Me,*

27 *and you will testify also, because you have been with Me from the beginning.*

DISCUSS with your GROUP or PONDER on your own . . .

Overview the Text

Describe the setting. Who is Jesus talking to? What topics does He address?

What repeating words did you notice?

John 15:1-17 Questions

What illustration does Jesus use in the opening verses of this section? Who do the vine, the vinedresser, and the two kinds of branches represent?

Week Four: **Words in the Upper Room**

Compare the two types of branches He describes. What do they have in common? How are they different?

What does the vinedresser do to the branches that bear fruit? Why?

The Greek word that translates "prunes" (*kathairo*) in verse 2 is the verb form of the adjective "clean" (*katharos*) in verse 3. How are the disciples already clean and what implication does this have for fruit bearing? Is this applicable to us? Explain.

What specific commands does Jesus make in this section? What promises does He make?

Based on your marking, list everything Jesus says about *abiding* in John 15:1-17.

What does *abide in the vine* mean? Why is abiding important in your life? Why are we able to abide?

What evidence does your life give of abiding in the Vine?

John 15:18-27

What can Christ's disciples expect from the world? Why?

ONE STEP FURTHER:

Word Study: Abide
If you have some extra time this week, find the Greek word and see how it is used elsewhere. Pay close attention to how John uses it not only in John 15 but also in his first epistle. Record your findings below.

What does Jesus tell His disciples to remember? How will this help them?

What does sin have to do with Jesus' work and the disciples' futures?
How do people typically respond when confronted with their sin? Why?

What else does Jesus say about the Helper in verses 26-27?
Who does He point to?

Who does the Holy Spirit point to today? How can this truth help us discern?

OBSERVE the TEXT of SCRIPTURE

READ John 16. **IDENTIFY** and **MARK** key repeating words. Also **MARK** time phrases you see throughout the chapter.

John 16

1   *"These things I have spoken to you so that you may be kept from stumbling.*

2   *"They will make you outcasts from the synagogue, but an hour is coming for everyone who kills you to think that he is offering service to God.*

3   *"These things they will do because they have not known the Father or Me.*

4   *"But these things I have spoken to you, so that when their hour comes, you may remember that I told you of them. These things I did not say to you at the beginning, because I was with you.*

5   *"But now I am going to Him who sent Me; and none of you asks Me, 'Where are You going?'*

6   *"But because I have said these things to you, sorrow has filled your heart.*

7   *"But I tell you the truth, it is to your advantage that I go away; for if I do not go away, the Helper will not come to you; but if I go, I will send Him to you.*

8   *"And He, when He comes, will convict the world concerning sin and righteousness and judgment;*

9   *concerning sin, because they do not believe in Me;*

10   *and concerning righteousness, because I go to the Father and you no longer see Me;*

11 and concerning judgment, because the ruler of this world has been judged.

12 "I have many more things to say to you, but you cannot bear them now.

13 "But when He, the Spirit of truth, comes, He will guide you into all the truth; for He will not speak on His own initiative, but whatever He hears, He will speak; and He will disclose to you what is to come.

14 "He will glorify Me, for He will take of Mine and will disclose it to you.

15 "All things that the Father has are Mine; therefore I said that He takes of Mine and will disclose it to you.

16 "A little while, and you will no longer see Me; and again a little while, and you will see Me."

17 Some of His disciples then said to one another, "What is this thing He is telling us, 'A little while, and you will not see Me; and again a little while, and you will see Me'; and, 'because I go to the Father'?"

18 So they were saying, "What is this that He says, 'A little while'? We do not know what He is talking about."

19 Jesus knew that they wished to question Him, and He said to them, "Are you deliberating together about this, that I said, 'A little while, and you will not see Me, and again a little while, and you will see Me'?

20 "Truly, truly, I say to you, that you will weep and lament, but the world will rejoice; you will grieve, but your grief will be turned into joy.

21 "Whenever a woman is in labor she has pain, because her hour has come; but when she gives birth to the child, she no longer remembers the anguish because of the joy that a child has been born into the world.

22 "Therefore you too have grief now; but I will see you again, and your heart will rejoice, and no one will take your joy away from you.

23 "In that day you will not question Me about anything. Truly, truly, I say to you, if you ask the Father for anything in My name, He will give it to you.

24 "Until now you have asked for nothing in My name; ask and you will receive, so that your joy may be made full.

25 "These things I have spoken to you in figurative language; an hour is coming when I will no longer speak to you in figurative language, but will tell you plainly of the Father.

26 "In that day you will ask in My name, and I do not say to you that I will request of the Father on your behalf;

27 for the Father Himself loves you, because you have loved Me and have believed that I came forth from the Father.

28 "I came forth from the Father and have come into the world; I am leaving the world again and going to the Father."

29 His disciples said, "Lo, now You are speaking plainly and are not using a figure of speech.

30 "Now we know that You know all things, and have no need for anyone to question You; by this we believe that You came from God."

31 *Jesus answered them, "Do you now believe?*

32 *"Behold, an hour is coming, and has already come, for you to be scattered, each to his own home, and to leave Me alone; and yet I am not alone, because the Father is with Me.*

33 *"These things I have spoken to you, so that in Me you may have peace. In the world you have tribulation, but take courage; I have overcome the world."*

DISCUSS with your GROUP or PONDER on your own . . .

Overview the Text

Summarize what Jesus has been talking about in John 14 and 15.

Where is His focus in John 16? What additional topics does He address?

What repeating words did you notice?

John 16:1-4 Questions

Jesus uses the pronoun *houtos* (translated "these things") three times in this section to refer to things He told the disciples. What was He referring to in each case and why or why not?

	What were "these things"	Why/why not spoken
16:1		
16:4a		
16:4b		

Week Four: **Words in the Upper Room**

What time phrases does Jesus use? What do they tell us about when events will happen?

What will Jesus' words do for the disciples? How does this apply to us as His disciples today?

Why does Jesus say He waited to tell the disciples some things?

What do the disciples need to do with the words Jesus has spoken? Are you doing this? Explain.

What does "remembering" presuppose?

John 16:5-15 Questions

What does Jesus say caused sorrow to fill the disciples' heart? (Keep your eye on "filled" and notice later in the chapter what will fill their hearts.) Is their sorrow based on truth? Explain.

What encouraging truth does Jesus give His disciples?

Who is the Helper? How is His arrival connected to Jesus' departure? What have we already learned about Him in John 14 and 15?

How will the Helper interact with the world? What three things will He do?

How do each of these relate to the person and work of Jesus? Consider John 15:22-27 as you answer.

Compile another short list of what the Holy Spirit will do for believers (include John 14:26 and 15:26).

According to the text, how is the Spirit's work tied to the person and work of Jesus Christ?

How has the Holy Spirit guided you in living out truth?

John 16:16-33 Questions

What do the disciples find confusing in verses 16-19?

How does Jesus explain Himself in the subsequent verses? What conflicting emotions will they experience? Which will last and why?

What else does Jesus say will happen in coming days that is positive in nature?

ONE STEP FURTHER:

When Tenses Matter

The Greek perfect tense indicates a past completed action with continuing results. If you're up for a challenge, use your study tools to identify Jesus' usage of the perfect tense in these chapters. Record your findings below.

Why will the disciples be able to ask anything of the Father? How are they to do it? What conditions come with asking "in My name"? What does this presuppose about relationship with the Father?

What else is on the horizon for the disciples according to verse 32?

Why does Jesus tell the disciples these things?

On what basis do we "take courage" in tribulation? How are you doing at believing and acting on this truth?

OBSERVE the TEXT of SCRIPTURE

READ John 17. **IDENTIFY** and **MARK** key repeating words. Be sure to include *truth*, *word*, and *world*.

John 17

1 *Jesus spoke these things; and lifting up His eyes to heaven, He said, "Father, the hour has come; glorify Your Son, that the Son may glorify You,*

2 *even as You gave Him authority over all flesh, that to all whom You have given Him, He may give eternal life.*

3 *"This is eternal life, that they may know You, the only true God, and Jesus Christ whom You have sent.*

4 *"I glorified You on the earth, having accomplished the work which You have given Me to do.*

5 *"Now, Father, glorify Me together with Yourself, with the glory which I had with You before the world was.*

6 *"I have manifested Your name to the men whom You gave Me out of the world; they were Yours and You gave them to Me, and they have kept Your word.*

7 *"Now they have come to know that everything You have given Me is from You;*

8 *for the words which You gave Me I have given to them; and they received them and truly understood that I came forth from You, and they believed that You sent Me.*

9 *"I ask on their behalf; I do not ask on behalf of the world, but of those whom You have given Me; for they are Yours;*

10 and all things that are Mine are Yours, and Yours are Mine; and I have been glorified in them.

11 "I am no longer in the world; and yet they themselves are in the world, and I come to You. Holy Father, keep them in Your name, the name which You have given Me, that they may be one even as We are.

12 "While I was with them, I was keeping them in Your name which You have given Me; and I guarded them and not one of them perished but the son of perdition, so that the Scripture would be fulfilled.

13 "But now I come to You; and these things I speak in the world so that they may have My joy made full in themselves.

14 "I have given them Your word; and the world has hated them, because they are not of the world, even as I am not of the world.

15 "I do not ask You to take them out of the world, but to keep them from the evil one.

16 "They are not of the world, even as I am not of the world.

17 "Sanctify them in the truth; Your word is truth.

18 "As You sent Me into the world, I also have sent them into the world.

19 "For their sakes I sanctify Myself, that they themselves also may be sanctified in truth.

20 "I do not ask on behalf of these alone, but for those also who believe in Me through their word;

21 that they may all be one; even as You, Father, are in Me and I in You, that they also may be in Us, so that the world may believe that You sent Me.

22 "The glory which You have given Me I have given to them, that they may be one, just as We are one;

23 I in them and You in Me, that they may be perfected in unity, so that the world may know that You sent Me, and loved them, even as You have loved Me.

24 "Father, I desire that they also, whom You have given Me, be with Me where I am, so that they may see My glory which You have given Me, for You loved Me before the foundation of the world.

25 "O righteous Father, although the world has not known You, yet I have known You; and these have known that You sent Me;

26 and I have made Your name known to them, and will make it known, so that the love with which You loved Me may be in them, and I in them."

> **FYI:**
>
> **Keep Them From the Evil One**
> When Jesus prays that the Father will "keep" His disciples from the evil one, He uses the Greek word *tereo*. The noun form of this verb means a warden or guard. In this case the sense of the verb is to keep safe, preserve, or take care of.

DISCUSS with your GROUP or PONDER on your own . . .

Overview the Text

Who is Jesus addressing in John 17? What main topics does He address?

VOICES
HEARING GOD
IN A WORLD OF
IMPOSTORS

Week Four: **Words in the Upper Room**

What key words did you identify?

John 17:1-12 Questions

What does Jesus pray for Himself in this section?

What does Jesus have the authority to give? To whom?

How does He define "eternal life"?

How did Jesus glorify the Father? How is your life bringing glory to the Father?

What key truths did Jesus' disciples believe about Him? How did they come to know these truths?

What does Jesus ask for His disciples? Why does He ask for this now?

John 17:13-26 Questions

When Jesus goes to the Father, how will the disciples be able to have joy?

What does Jesus say about the world? (You could make a list!) What is the disposition of the world toward His disciples?

How are the disciples supposed to interact with the world? What does Jesus ask the Father to do for them with regard to the world?

How are you doing at being "in" the world but not "of" it? What specific challenges are you encountering in your household?

What does Jesus ask the Father to do for His disciples with regard to truth? How does He define truth?

Who else does He pray for according to verses 21-22?

How will others come to believe?

How will the disciples' behavior point to the truth that the Father sent Jesus into the world? Does your life do this? How?

Is real unity possible apart from truth? Explain your answer.

Week Four: **Words in the Upper Room**

How far back does the love between the Father and the Son extend?

How is Christian love shown in your church? How does this differ from "love" in other organizations?

Digging Deeper

Good Shepherds and Bad Shepherds

Finally, take some time to study through John 10 where Jesus talks about good shepherds, bad shepherds, and sheep who know the difference. In order to pick up the context, start by reading John 9.

Who is Jesus talking to in John 10?

In what context does He talk about the shepherds and the sheep? Why is he using this particular illustration?

How does the Good Shepherd differ from others who deal with the sheep?

Where specifically are the sheep following the Good Shepherd's voice to?

Why didn't *the Jews* He was talking to believe Him?

Why do *you* believe Him?

@THE END OF THE DAY . . .

Thinking back through John 14–17, summarize how Jesus equipped His disciples for His departure. As you work through this, be sure to include topics He addressed, commands He gave, and prayers He prayed on their behalf and ours. Based on this, what should you be focused on? How are you doing with this?

Week Four: **Words in the Upper Room**

Empowered by the Spirit

"It is not for you to know times or epochs which the Father has fixed by His own authority; but you will receive power when the Holy Spirit has come upon you; and you shall be My witnesses both in Jerusalem, and in all Judea and Samaria, and even to the remotest part of the earth."
—Jesus, Acts 1:7-8

The narrative book of Acts confronts Christians with live-it-out-in-the-here-and-now issues that fundamentally impact how believers walk by faith and live out their salvation with fear and trembling.

As we look at the text of Acts inductively, we'll wrestle with two fundamental questions:

1. When is Acts to be interpreted descriptively and when is it to be interpreted prescriptively? In other words, when does Acts primarily describe what happened as God grew the first century church and when does it teach us to emulate behaviors or practices?

The second question has to do with how we interpret the baptism of the Holy Spirit.

2. Is it normative for the baptism of the Holy Spirit to take place at conversion or some time later? Viewing the baptism of the Holy Spirit as an event secondary to regeneration changes how many texts will apply.

Where people land on each of these questions will affect their interpretation of other passages and ultimately will impact the way they pursue God. Will they pursue Him through His Word or will they seek visions, miracles, signs, and wonders?

As we begin this week, we will look at Acts 2 which recounts the coming of the Holy Spirit at Pentecost and then three subsequent and similar events. As we move into this portion of our study, it's critical to stick to the text of Scripture and walk with grace in our interactions if we encounter points of disagreement.

SETTING THE SCENE

Before Jesus ascends to the Father, He tells His disciples that they "will be baptized with the Holy Spirit not many days from now" (v. 5 below).

FYI:

Authorship
It is widely held that Luke the physician is the author of both the Gospel of Luke and the Acts of the Apostles.

Week Five: **Empowered by the Spirit**

OBSERVE the TEXT of SCRIPTURE

READ Acts 1:1-8. **MARK** every reference to the *Holy Spirit* and to *baptized*.

Acts 1:1-8

1   *The first account I composed, Theophilus, about all that Jesus began to do and teach,*

2   *until the day when He was taken up to heaven, after He had by the Holy Spirit given orders to the apostles whom He had chosen.*

3   *To these He also presented Himself alive after His suffering, by many convincing proofs, appearing to them over a period of forty days and speaking of the things concerning the kingdom of God.*

4   *Gathering them together, He commanded them not to leave Jerusalem, but to wait for what the Father had promised, "Which," He said, "you heard of from Me;*

5   *for John baptized with water, but you will be baptized with the Holy Spirit not many days from now."*

6   *So when they had come together, they were asking Him, saying, "Lord, is it at this time You are restoring the kingdom to Israel?"*

7   *He said to them, "It is not for you to know times or epochs which the Father has fixed by His own authority;*

8   *but you will receive power when the Holy Spirit has come upon you; and you shall be My witnesses both in Jerusalem, and in all Judea and Samaria, and even to the remotest part of the earth."*

DISCUSS with your GROUP or PONDER on your own . . .

Who is the author writing to? What had he written about in his first account?

What does he say about Jesus' post-resurrection appearances? Who had He appeared to? Over how long a time frame?

What does Jesus command the disciples to wait for in Jerusalem? What will they receive? What will they become?

How are you doing at being His witness in your sphere of influence? Are you living as a witness by the power of the Spirit? Explain.

SETTING THE SCENE

After Jesus ascends to the Father, the disciples obey Him by waiting in Jerusalem for the Spirit to come.

OBSERVE the TEXT of SCRIPTURE

READ Acts 2. **MARK** references to the *Holy Spirit* and also to all sound-related words.

Acts 2

1 When the day of Pentecost had come, they were all together in one place.

2 And suddenly there came from heaven a noise like a violent rushing wind, and it filled the whole house where they were sitting.

3 And there appeared to them tongues as of fire distributing themselves, and they rested on each one of them.

4 And they were all filled with the Holy Spirit and began to speak with other tongues, as the Spirit was giving them utterance.

5 Now there were Jews living in Jerusalem, devout men from every nation under heaven.

6 And when this sound occurred, the crowd came together, and were bewildered because each one of them was hearing them speak in his own language.

7 They were amazed and astonished, saying, "Why, are not all these who are speaking Galileans?

8 "And how is it that we each hear them in our own language to which we were born?

9 "Parthians and Medes and Elamites, and residents of Mesopotamia, Judea and Cappadocia, Pontus and Asia,

10 Phrygia and Pamphylia, Egypt and the districts of Libya around Cyrene, and visitors from Rome, both Jews and proselytes,

11 Cretans and Arabs—we hear them in our own tongues speaking of the mighty deeds of God."

12 And they all continued in amazement and great perplexity, saying to one another, "What does this mean?"

13 But others were mocking and saying, "They are full of sweet wine."

14 But Peter, taking his stand with the eleven, raised his voice and declared to them: "Men of Judea and all you who live in Jerusalem, let this be known to you and give heed to my words.

FYI:

Baptize
The word for baptize in Greek is *baptizo* which literally means to dip or immerse, to wash or purify, and in some cases to dye.

VOICES
HEARING GOD
IN A WORLD OF
IMPOSTORS

New Testament

ONE STEP FURTHER:

Joel's Prophecy

When Peter preaches at Pentecost, he asserts that the prophet Joel's words are being fulfilled. In order to better understand the context, take some time this week to read the three-chapter book of Joel and record your observations below.

15 *"For these men are not drunk, as you suppose, for it is only the third hour of the day;*

16 *but this is what was spoken of through the prophet Joel:*

17 *'AND IT SHALL BE IN THE LAST DAYS,' God says,*

'THAT I WILL POUR FORTH OF MY SPIRIT ON ALL MANKIND;

AND YOUR SONS AND YOUR DAUGHTERS SHALL PROPHESY,

AND YOUR YOUNG MEN SHALL SEE VISIONS,

AND YOUR OLD MEN SHALL DREAM DREAMS;

18 *EVEN ON MY BONDSLAVES, BOTH MEN AND WOMEN,*

I WILL IN THOSE DAYS POUR FORTH OF MY SPIRIT

And they shall prophesy.

19 *'AND I WILL GRANT WONDERS IN THE SKY ABOVE*

AND SIGNS ON THE EARTH BELOW,

BLOOD, AND FIRE, AND VAPOR OF SMOKE.

20 *'THE SUN WILL BE TURNED INTO DARKNESS*

AND THE MOON INTO BLOOD,

BEFORE THE GREAT AND GLORIOUS DAY OF THE LORD SHALL COME.

21 *'AND IT SHALL BE THAT EVERYONE WHO CALLS ON THE NAME OF THE LORD WILL BE SAVED.'*

22 *"Men of Israel, listen to these words: Jesus the Nazarene, a man attested to you by God with miracles and wonders and signs which God performed through Him in your midst, just as you yourselves know—*

23 *this Man, delivered over by the predetermined plan and foreknowledge of God, you nailed to a cross by the hands of godless men and put Him to death.*

24 *"But God raised Him up again, putting an end to the agony of death, since it was impossible for Him to be held in its power.*

25 *"For David says of Him,*

'I SAW THE LORD ALWAYS IN MY PRESENCE;

FOR HE IS AT MY RIGHT HAND, SO THAT I WILL NOT BE SHAKEN.

26 *'THEREFORE MY HEART WAS GLAD AND MY TONGUE EXULTED;*

MOREOVER MY FLESH ALSO WILL LIVE IN HOPE;

27 *BECAUSE YOU WILL NOT ABANDON MY SOUL TO HADES,*

NOR ALLOW YOUR HOLY ONE TO UNDERGO DECAY.

28 *'YOU HAVE MADE KNOWN TO ME THE WAYS OF LIFE;*

YOU WILL MAKE ME FULL OF GLADNESS WITH YOUR PRESENCE.'

29 *"Brethren, I may confidently say to you regarding the patriarch David that he both died and was buried, and his tomb is with us to this day.*

30   *"And so, because he was a prophet and knew that GOD HAD SWORN TO HIM WITH AN OATH TO SEAT one OF HIS DESCENDANTS ON HIS THRONE,*

31   *he looked ahead and spoke of the resurrection of the Christ, that HE WAS NEITHER ABANDONED TO HADES, NOR DID His flesh SUFFER DECAY.*

32   *"This Jesus God raised up again, to which we are all witnesses.*

33   *"Therefore having been exalted to the right hand of God, and having received from the Father the promise of the Holy Spirit, He has poured forth this which you both see and hear.*

34   *"For it was not David who ascended into heaven, but he himself says:*

'THE LORD SAID TO MY LORD,

"SIT AT MY RIGHT HAND,

35   *UNTIL I MAKE YOUR ENEMIES A FOOTSTOOL FOR YOUR FEET." '*

36   *"Therefore let all the house of Israel know for certain that God has made Him both Lord and Christ—this Jesus whom you crucified."*

37   *Now when they heard this, they were pierced to the heart, and said to Peter and the rest of the apostles, "Brethren, what shall we do?"*

38   *Peter said to them, "Repent, and each of you be baptized in the name of Jesus Christ for the forgiveness of your sins; and you will receive the gift of the Holy Spirit.*

39   *"For the promise is for you and your children and for all who are far off, as many as the Lord our God will call to Himself."*

40   *And with many other words he solemnly testified and kept on exhorting them, saying, "Be saved from this perverse generation!"*

41   *So then, those who had received his word were baptized; and that day there were added about three thousand souls.*

42   *They were continually devoting themselves to the apostles' teaching and to fellowship, to the breaking of bread and to prayer.*

43   *Everyone kept feeling a sense of awe; and many wonders and signs were taking place through the apostles.*

44   *And all those who had believed were together and had all things in common;*

45   *and they began selling their property and possessions and were sharing them with all, as anyone might have need.*

46   *Day by day continuing with one mind in the temple, and breaking bread from house to house, they were taking their meals together with gladness and sincerity of heart,*

47   *praising God and having favor with all the people. And the Lord was adding to their number day by day those who were being saved.*

ONE STEP FURTHER:

The Holy Spirit

Looking back at every place you marked Holy Spirit in Acts 2, compile a list on the third person of the Trinity from this chapter.

DISCUSS with your GROUP or PONDER on your own . . .

What people are involved in the event on Pentecost in Jerusalem? How are they the same? In what ways do they differ?

VOICES

HEARING GOD
IN A WORLD OF
IMPOSTORS

New Testament

Week Five: **Empowered by the Spirit**

Describe the coming of the Spirit.

What do the disciples hear? What do they see? What do they do?

What does the crowd hear? How do they respond?

What is declared? Is it clear? Explain.

What do the mockers say?

How does Peter defend the scene and show it as fulfilled prophecy from Scripture?

Has all of Joel's prophecy that Peter quotes been fulfilled? What does the text say?

How is the scope of the ministry of the Holy Spirit changing? What was it in the Old Testament? How is it different now?

During the time of Joel's writing, what people did God typically speak to?

What ways were the Jews accustomed to hearing Him speak? (Think through Old Testament accounts. Also consider Hebrews 1:1.)

What does Peter say about "miracles and wonders and signs" in verse 22?

What is the main point of his sermon? How does it affect his hearers?

What does he call people to do in verse 38? What will they receive?

What was taking place in verse 43? Through whom specifically? (See also 2 Corinthians 12:12 and Hebrews 2:1-4.)

SETTING THE SCENE

In the beginning of Acts 8 Philip proclaims Christ in Samaria. When the people accept the message, Peter and John come to town.

ONE STEP FURTHER:

Authenticating the Apostles

Hebrews exalts the great salvation "spoken through the Lord" and shows the enormous liability of rejecting it.

For this reason we must pay much closer attention to what we have heard, so that we do not drift away from it.

For if the word spoken through angels proved unalterable, and every transgression and disobedience received a just penalty, how will we escape if we neglect so great a salvation? After it was at the first spoken through the Lord, it was confirmed to us by those who heard,

God also testifying with them, both by signs and wonders and by various miracles and by gifts of the Holy Spirit according to His own will.

—Hebrew 2:1-4

- What word were the Hebrews not to drift from?

- What can they expect if they do drift?

- Who had spoken it first?

- Who spoke it next? Who were "those who heard"?

- Who did God testify with "by signs and wonders and by various miracles"?

- Why did God testify with them? What was the purpose?

- Is there any indication that we should seek signs and wonders today?

VOICES
HEARING GOD
IN A WORLD OF
IMPOSTORS

ONE STEP FURTHER:

Samaria Snapshots

For a little more cultural background on Samaritans, check out John 4 where Jesus talks to the woman at the well in Samaria and Luke 15 where Jesus tells the parable of the Good Samaritan. Record what you learn from each below.

John 4

Luke 10:25-37

OBSERVE the TEXT of SCRIPTURE

READ Acts 8:14-25. **MARK** in a distinctive way all references to the *Holy Spirit* and *prayer*. Also **MARK** phrases which refer to the *laying on of hands*.

Acts 8:14-25

14 *Now when the apostles in Jerusalem heard that Samaria had received the word of God, they sent them Peter and John,*

15 *who came down and prayed for them that they might receive the Holy Spirit.*

16 *For He had not yet fallen upon any of them; they had simply been baptized in the name of the Lord Jesus.*

17 *Then they began laying their hands on them, and they were receiving the Holy Spirit.*

18 *Now when Simon saw that the Spirit was bestowed through the laying on of the apostles' hands, he offered them money,*

19 *saying, "Give this authority to me as well, so that everyone on whom I lay my hands may receive the Holy Spirit."*

20 *But Peter said to him, "May your silver perish with you, because you thought you could obtain the gift of God with money!*

21 *"You have no part or portion in this matter, for your heart is not right before God.*

22 *"Therefore repent of this wickedness of yours, and pray the Lord that, if possible, the intention of your heart may be forgiven you.*

23 *"For I see that you are in the gall of bitterness and in the bondage of iniquity."*

24 *But Simon answered and said, "Pray to the Lord for me yourselves, so that nothing of what you have said may come upon me."*

25 *So, when they had solemnly testified and spoken the word of the Lord, they started back to Jerusalem, and were preaching the gospel to many villages of the Samaritans.*

DISCUSS with your GROUP or PONDER on your own . . .

Who receives the word of God, according to verse 14? Was this surprising? Explain.

Why are Peter and John sent? What is notable about them?

What had happened to the people? What hadn't happened yet?

What happened when the Apostles laid hands on the Samaritans? What potential abuse reared its head? How did Peter deal with it?

What does this passage teach about the Holy Spirit? Compile a short list.

SETTING THE SCENE

In Acts 11, Peter summarizes for the Jewish brethren in Jerusalem the events that took place when God led him to bring the Gospel to Gentiles.

OBSERVE the TEXT of SCRIPTURE

READ Acts 11:1-18. **MARK** distinctively every occurrence of *voice*, *word*, and *the Holy Spirit.*

Acts 11:1-18

1   Now the apostles and the brethren who were throughout Judea heard that the Gentiles also had received the word of God.

2   And when Peter came up to Jerusalem, those who were circumcised took issue with him,

3   saying, "You went to uncircumcised men and ate with them."

4   But Peter began speaking and proceeded to explain to them in orderly sequence, saying,

5   "I was in the city of Joppa praying; and in a trance I saw a vision, an object coming down like a great sheet lowered by four corners from the sky; and it came right down to me,

6   and when I had fixed my gaze on it and was observing it I saw the four-footed animals of the earth and the wild beasts and the crawling creatures and the birds of the air.

7   "I also heard a voice saying to me, 'Get up, Peter; kill and eat.'

8   "But I said, 'By no means, Lord, for nothing unholy or unclean has ever entered my mouth.'

9   "But a voice from heaven answered a second time, 'What God has cleansed, no longer consider unholy.'

10   "This happened three times, and everything was drawn back up into the sky.

11   "And behold, at that moment three men appeared at the house in which we were staying, having been sent to me from Caesarea.

12   "The Spirit told me to go with them without misgivings. These six brethren also went with me and we entered the man's house.

ONE STEP FURTHER:

Spiritual Abusers

As bad shepherds do not care for sheep and as wolves sneak in among them, Simon had an interest in God's power but not in God Himself, wanting to buy with money the authority (Greek: *excusia*, also power or right) to dispense the Holy Spirit personally. Simon may sound crazy to you as you read the account . . . but have you seen modern Simons? What avenues of abuse fly open when people think they are and/or claim to be dispensers of spiritual power? What biblical truths reign over this kind of thinking?

VOICES
HEARING GOD
IN A WORLD OF
IMPOSTORS

Week Five: **Empowered by the Spirit**

13 "And he reported to us how he had seen the angel standing in his house, and saying, 'Send to Joppa and have Simon, who is also called Peter, brought here;

14 and he will speak words to you by which you will be saved, you and all your household.'

15 "And as I began to speak, the Holy Spirit fell upon them just as He did upon us at the beginning.

16 "And I remembered the word of the Lord, how He used to say, 'John baptized with water, but you will be baptized with the Holy Spirit.'

17 "Therefore if God gave to them the same gift as He gave to us also after believing in the Lord Jesus Christ, who was I that I could stand in God's way?"

18 When they heard this, they quieted down and glorified God, saying, "Well then, God has granted to the Gentiles also the repentance that leads to life."

DISCUSS with your GROUP or PONDER on your own . . .

What are Peter's Jewish brethren upset about? Why? How does Peter relate his vision to the situation?

What does the Spirit tell Peter to do with regard to the visitors? What does the Spirit tell Cornelius to do? (Acts 10 tells us that Cornelius is the man referred to in Acts 11:12-13.)

How does the Spirit authenticate His own message?

What happens when Peter speaks? What does he remember?

What had the Gentiles received? How was this related to Peter's vision? (Look carefully at the whole section.)

Were the Jewish brethren expecting the Gospel to go to the Gentiles? Explain your answer from the text. Could they deny that it had? Again, explain your answer.

SETTING THE SCENE

Up to this point, the Spirit has come to the disciples as Jesus promised At Pentecost when the Holy Spirit is poured out, the Gospel is proclaimed to the Jews in their own dialects. Later the coming of the Spirit confirms that the Gospel has been received by the half-breed Samaritans and then the Gentiles. In this final record of the Spirit being poured out, those on whom the Spirit falls are called "disciples." The question is: *Whose disciples?* Let's look at text.

OBSERVE the TEXT of SCRIPTURE

READ Acts 19:1-7. **MARK** in a distinct way references to *baptism, the Holy Spirit,* and *disciples.*

Acts 19:1-7

1 *It happened that while Apollos was at Corinth, Paul passed through the upper country and came to Ephesus, and found some disciples.*

2 *He said to them, "Did you receive the Holy Spirit when you believed?" And they said to him, "No, we have not even heard whether there is a Holy Spirit."*

3 *And he said, "Into what then were you baptized?" And they said. "Into John's baptism."*

4 *Paul said, "John baptized with the baptism of repentance, telling the people to believe in Him who was coming after him, that is, in Jesus."*

5 *When they heard this, they were baptized in the name of the Lord Jesus.*

6 *And when Paul had laid his hands upon them, the Holy Spirit came on them, and they began speaking with tongues and prophesying.*

7 *There were in all about twelve men.*

DISCUSS with your GROUP or PONDER on your own . . .

Where is Paul? Describe the "disciples" he finds.

What do they already believe? What do they still need to believe?

Week Five: **Empowered by the Spirit**

What does the text tell us about the Holy Spirit?

Based on this and other biblical texts, when did these people come to faith in Christ? Explain.

Midweek Wrap-Up . . .

Take a few minutes to summarize what you've learned so far this week about the workings of the Holy Spirit in the early chapters of Acts. Is this consistent with what you have been assuming about His work or have your preconceptions and opinions been altered? What has been your most significant takeaway with regard to how the Holy Spirit worked in the early Church and how He works in our lives today?

PETER's EXPERIENCES and PETER's INSTRUCTIONS

One of the most prominent disciples in the Gospels, Peter is also a leading figure in the book of Acts. Present at three of four events where the Spirit falls on different groups of people, Peter not only witnessed Jesus' life and ministry, he was also up close and personal to the Spirit's establishing the early Church.

Want to talk about experiences? Peter had them. He was there for the tongues of fire. When he preached, thousands received Christ. He healed the lame. For Pete's sake (couldn't resist!) he raised the dead in the name of Jesus. He saw visions, heard voices and even had an angel spring him from prison—twice! If anyone had reason to point people to signs and wonders on the basis of personal experience, it was Peter.

We've already looked at three accounts where Peter is right in the middle of God's expansion of His Church: the pouring out of the Spirit on Jewish believers, then Samaritans, then Gentiles. Let's take a look together at a few more supernatural experiences that Luke records in the book of Acts. Then, we'll look at Peter's writings (1 and 2 Peter) to see how Peter himself, moved by the Holy Spirit, told Christ's followers to seek Him.

PETER's EXPERIENCES
SETTING THE SCENE: Acts 5:1-21

As many believing landowners are selling property and bringing it to the apostles to help meet the needs of others, Ananias and Sapphira join the movement in the

OBSERVE the TEXT of SCRIPTURE

READ Acts 5:1-11. **MARK** every reference to *Ananias* and *Sapphira*, including pronouns.

Acts 5:1-11

1 But a man named Ananias, with his wife Sapphira, sold a piece of property,

2 and kept back some of the price for himself, with his wife's full knowledge, and bringing a portion of it, he laid it at the apostles' feet.

3 But Peter said, "Ananias, why has Satan filled your heart to lie to the Holy Spirit and to keep back some of the price of the land?

4 "While it remained unsold, did it not remain your own? And after it was sold, was it not under your control? Why is it that you have conceived this deed in your heart? You have not lied to men but to God."

5 And as he heard these words, Ananias fell down and breathed his last; and great fear came over all who heard of it.

6 The young men got up and covered him up, and after carrying him out, they buried him.

7 Now there elapsed an interval of about three hours, and his wife came in, not knowing what had happened.

8 And Peter responded to her, "Tell me whether you sold the land for such and such a price?" And she said, "Yes, that was the price."

9 Then Peter said to her, "Why is it that you have agreed together to put the Spirit of the Lord to the test? Behold, the feet of those who have buried your husband are at the door, and they will carry you out as well."

10 And immediately she fell at his feet and breathed her last, and the young men came in and found her dead, and they carried her out and buried her beside her husband.

11 And great fear came over the whole church, and over all who heard of these things.

DISCUSS with your GROUP or PONDER on your own . . .

Describe Ananias and Sapphira. Where did they get the money they brought to the Apostles? What information do they hold back from them?

What does Peter ask Ananias? What does Peter accuse Ananias of? What happens to Ananias?

Week Five: **Empowered by the Spirit**

What does Peter ask Ananias's wife? How does she respond? What happens to her?

Although the text is not crystal clear on this one, how do you think Peter learned about their agreement to conspire? Defend your view.

OBSERVE the TEXT of SCRIPTURE

READ Acts 5:12-16. **MARK** every reference to *the apostles* and *Peter* including pronouns.

Acts 5:12-16

12 *At the hands of the apostles many signs and wonders were taking place among the people; and they were all with one accord in Solomon's portico.*

13 *But none of the rest dared to associate with them; however, the people held them in high esteem.*

14 *And all the more believers in the Lord, multitudes of men and women, were constantly added to their number,*

15 *to such an extent that they even carried the sick out into the streets and laid them on cots and pallets, so that when Peter came by at least his shadow might fall on any one of them.*

16 *Also the people from the cities in the vicinity of Jerusalem were coming together, bringing people who were sick or afflicted with unclean spirits, and they were all being healed.*

DISCUSS with your GROUP or PONDER on your own . . .

Who performed signs and wonders in this scenario? What specific miracles occurred?

What affect did the signs and wonders have on the people? On their view of the Apostles? On their behavior? Explain.

OBSERVE the TEXT of SCRIPTURE

READ Acts 5:17-21. Then, in the text below, **MARK** references to *an angel of the Lord*, including pronouns.

Acts 5:17-21

17 But the high priest rose up, along with all his associates (that is the sect of the Sadducees), and they were filled with jealousy.

18 They laid hands on the apostles and put them in a public jail.

19 But during the night an angel of the Lord opened the gates of the prison, and taking them out he said,

20 "Go, stand and speak to the people in the temple the whole message of this Life."

21 Upon hearing this, *they* entered into the temple about daybreak and began to teach.

DISCUSS with your GROUP or PONDER on your own . . .

What lands the Apostles in jail?

Describe the angel. When does he show up? What does he do? What does he say to the Apostles?

How do they respond? What does Peter go on to teach in subsequent verses?

A DECISION-MAKING SHIFT
SETTING THE SCENE

It's hard to deny the in-your-face clarity of God's dealings with Peter in the book of Acts. In addition to likely giving him insider information on Ananias and Sapphira, God specifically and unmistakably teaches Peter that Gentiles are clean by giving him a vision three times before commanding him to locate Cornelius. Still, when we look at two different decision-making situations Peter was involved with—one as Acts opens and the other in Acts 15, the last place we hear about Peter in the book—we see two different ways the disciples approached critical decisions regarding the direction of the Church. Let's take a look!

OBSERVE the TEXT of SCRIPTURE

READ Acts 1:15-26. **MARK** every reference to *God* in the text.

Acts 1:15-26

15 *At this time Peter stood up in the midst of the brethren (a gathering of about one hundred and twenty persons was there together), and said,*

16 *"Brethren, the Scripture had to be fulfilled, which the Holy Spirit foretold by the mouth of David concerning Judas, who became a guide to those who arrested Jesus.*

Digging Deeper

All About Peter

If you have extra time this week, read Acts 1–15 and summarize all the supernatural events in Peter's life. Consider when the Holy Spirit falls on people, when angels appear, when Peter has visions, hears voices, etc.

17 *"For he was counted among us and received his share in this ministry."*

18 *(Now this man acquired a field with the price of his wickedness, and falling headlong, he burst open in the middle and all his intestines gushed out.*

19 *And it became known to all who were living in Jerusalem; so that in their own language that field was called Hakeldama, that is, Field of Blood.)*

20 *"For it is written in the book of Psalms,*

   'LET HIS HOMESTEAD BE MADE DESOLATE,

   AND LET NO ONE DWELL IN IT';

   and,

   'LET ANOTHER MAN TAKE HIS OFFICE.'

21 *"Therefore it is necessary that of the men who have accompanied us all the time that the Lord Jesus went in and out among us—*

22 *beginning with the baptism of John until the day that He was taken up from us—one of these must become a witness with us of His resurrection."*

23 *So they put forward two men, Joseph called Barsabbas (who was also called Justus), and Matthias.*

24 *And they prayed and said, "You, Lord, who know the hearts of all men, show which one of these two You have chosen*

25 *to occupy this ministry and apostleship from which Judas turned aside to go to his own place."*

26 *And they drew lots for them, and the lot fell to Matthias; and he was added to the eleven apostles.*

DISCUSS with your GROUP or PONDER on your own . . .

What decision are the believers facing?

When does this happen in relation to the ascension of Jesus and the coming of the Holy Spirit?

What criteria do they use to come to up with candidates?

How does God play into their final decision-making process?

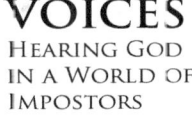

Week Five: **Empowered by the Spirit**

Is there Old Testament precedent for this? Explain.

SETTING THE SCENE

Before the coming of the Holy Spirit, the decision for Judas's replacement was made by praying and casting lots—the last lot-casting reference in the Bible. When the Jerusalem Council rolls around in Acts 15 and the Apostles face another major decision-making event, an entirely different scenario unfolds.

OBSERVE the TEXT of SCRIPTURE

READ Acts 15:1-29. **MARK** every reference to *the apostles and elders.*

Acts 15:1-29

1 *Some men came down from Judea and began teaching the brethren, "Unless you are circumcised according to the custom of Moses, you cannot be saved."*

2 *And when Paul and Barnabas had great dissension and debate with them, the brethren determined that Paul and Barnabas and some others of them should go up to Jerusalem to the apostles and elders concerning this issue.*

3 *Therefore, being sent on their way by the church, they were passing through both Phoenicia and Samaria, describing in detail the conversion of the Gentiles, and were bringing great joy to all the brethren.*

4 *When they arrived at Jerusalem, they were received by the church and the apostles and the elders, and they reported all that God had done with them.*

5 *But some of the sect of the Pharisees who had believed stood up, saying, "It is necessary to circumcise them and to direct them to observe the Law of Moses."*

6 *The apostles and the elders came together to look into this matter.*

7 *After there had been much debate, Peter stood up and said to them, "Brethren, you know that in the early days God made a choice among you, that by my mouth the Gentiles would hear the word of the gospel and believe.*

8 *"And God, who knows the heart, testified to them giving them the Holy Spirit, just as He also did to us;*

9 *and He made no distinction between us and them, cleansing their hearts by faith.*

10 *"Now therefore why do you put God to the test by placing upon the neck of the disciples a yoke which neither our fathers nor we have been able to bear?*

11 *"But we believe that we are saved through the grace of the Lord Jesus, in the same way as they also are."*

12 *All the people kept silent, and they were listening to Barnabas and Paul as they were relating what signs and wonders God had done through them among the Gentiles.*

13 *After they had stopped speaking, James answered, saying, "Brethren, listen to me.*

14 *"Simeon has related how God first concerned Himself about taking from among the Gentiles a people for His name.*

15 *"With this the words of the Prophets agree, just as it is written,*

16 *'AFTER THESE THINGS I will return,*

   AND I WILL REBUILD THE TABERNACLE OF DAVID WHICH HAS FALLEN,

   AND I WILL REBUILD ITS RUINS,

   AND I WILL RESTORE IT,

17 *SO THAT THE REST OF MANKIND MAY SEEK THE LORD,*

   AND ALL THE GENTILES WHO ARE CALLED BY MY NAME,'

18 *SAYS THE LORD, WHO MAKES THESE THINGS KNOWN FROM LONG AGO.*

19 *"Therefore it is my judgment that we do not trouble those who are turning to God from among the Gentiles,*

20 *but that we write to them that they abstain from things contaminated by idols and from fornication and from what is strangled and from blood.*

21 *"For Moses from ancient generations has in every city those who preach him, since he is read in the synagogues every Sabbath."*

22 *Then it seemed good to the apostles and the elders, with the whole church, to choose men from among them to send to Antioch with Paul and Barnabas—Judas called Barsabbas, and Silas, leading men among the brethren,*

23 *and they sent this letter by them,*

   "The apostles and the brethren who are elders, to the brethren in Antioch and Syria and Cilicia who are from the Gentiles, greetings.

24 *"Since we have heard that some of our number to whom we gave no instruction have disturbed you with their words, unsettling your souls,*

25 *it seemed good to us, having become of one mind, to select men to send to you with our beloved Barnabas and Paul,*

26 *men who have risked their lives for the name of our Lord Jesus Christ.*

27 *"Therefore we have sent Judas and Silas, who themselves will also report the same things by word of mouth.*

28 *"For it seemed good to the Holy Spirit and to us to lay upon you no greater burden than these essentials:*

29 *that you abstain from things sacrificed to idols and from blood and from things strangled and from fornication; if you keep yourselves free from such things, you will do well. Farewell."*

Week Five: **Empowered by the Spirit**

DISCUSS with your GROUP or PONDER on your own . . .

What is the big issue in Acts 15?

What are the different points of view and who is associated with each?

What do Paul and Barnabas describe for the Apostles and elders? What does this have to do with the issue?

What does Peter say about God's dealings with Gentiles? What point does he make?

How does James weigh the information? How does the council come to a decision?

Where in the passage does the Holy Spirit appear and what role does He play?

How does this differ from the decision-making in Acts 1?

What lessons can we learn from the Apostles' decision-making process? Explain.

SETTING THE SCENE

We learn much about Peter's life in the Gospel accounts as well as in Luke's Acts of the Apostles. Many scholars believe that Mark's Gospel is written largely from Peter's perspective. The two letters we have directly from Peter are 1 and 2 Peter. Let's see what he has to tell us. We'll be reading the entire letters—5 and 3 chapters respectively—and looking more closely as some excerpted segments.

OBSERVE the TEXT of SCRIPTURE

READ 1 Peter 1–2 in its entirety. In the section below, **UNDERLINE** commands Peter makes, both positive and negative.

1 Peter 1:13–2:3

13 *Therefore, prepare your minds for action, keep sober in spirit, fix your hope completely on the grace to be brought to you at the revelation of Jesus Christ.*

14 *As obedient children, do not be conformed to the former lusts which were yours in your ignorance,*

15 *but like the Holy One who called you, be holy yourselves also in all your behavior;*

16 *because it is written, "YOU SHALL BE HOLY, FOR I AM HOLY."*

17 *If you address as Father the One who impartially judges according to each one's work, conduct yourselves in fear during the time of your stay on earth;*

18 *knowing that you were not redeemed with perishable things like silver or gold from your futile way of life inherited from your forefathers,*

19 *but with precious blood, as of a lamb unblemished and spotless, the blood of Christ.*

20 *For He was foreknown before the foundation of the world, but has appeared in these last times for the sake of you*

21 *who through Him are believers in God, who raised Him from the dead and gave Him glory, so that your faith and hope are in God.*

22 *Since you have in obedience to the truth purified your souls for a sincere love of the brethren, fervently love one another from the heart,*

23 *for you have been born again not of seed which is perishable but imperishable, that is, through the living and enduring word of God.*

24 *For,*

"ALL FLESH IS LIKE GRASS,

AND ALL ITS GLORY LIKE THE FLOWER OF GRASS.

THE GRASS WITHERS,

AND THE FLOWER FALLS OFF,

25 *BUT THE WORD OF THE LORD ENDURES FOREVER."*

And this is the word which was preached to you.

1 *Therefore, putting aside all malice and all deceit and hypocrisy and envy and all slander,*

2 *like newborn babies, long for the pure milk of the word, so that by it you may grow in respect to salvation,*

3 *if you have tasted the kindness of the Lord.*

DISCUSS with your GROUP or PONDER on your own . . .

What does Peter tell his readers to do? To not do?

What does he say about the Word of God? What does he compare it to? How long does it last?

How can his readers grow in respect to salvation?

Have you been trying to grow in respect to salvation other ways? If so, what ways? Where have your growth instructions come from?

OBSERVE the TEXT of SCRIPTURE

READ all of 1 Peter 3–5. Then, in the text below **UNDERLINE** the commands Peter makes.

1 Peter 4:7-11

7 *The end of all things is near; therefore, be of sound judgment and sober spirit for the purpose of prayer.*

8 *Above all, keep fervent in your love for one another, because love covers a multitude of sins.*

9 *Be hospitable to one another without complaint.*

10 *As each one has received a special gift, employ it in serving one another as good stewards of the manifold grace of God.*

11 *Whoever speaks, is to do so as one who is speaking the utterances of God; whoever serves is to do so as one who is serving by the strength which God supplies; so that in all things God may be glorified through Jesus Christ, to whom belongs the glory and dominion forever and ever. Amen.*

1 Peter 5:8-11

8 *Be of sober spirit, be on the alert. Your adversary, the devil, prowls around like a roaring lion, seeking someone to devour.*

9 *But resist him, firm in your faith, knowing that the same experiences of suffering are being accomplished by your brethren who are in the world.*

10 *After you have suffered for a little while, the God of all grace, who called you to His eternal glory in Christ, will Himself perfect, confirm, strengthen and establish you.*

11 *To Him be dominion forever and ever. Amen.*

DISCUSS with your GROUP or PONDER on your own . . .

Again, what does Peter tell his readers to do? To not do?

What are Christ's followers to guard against?

What kind of threat does the adversary pose? How can we resist?

How are you doing at standing firm this week?

OBSERVE the TEXT of SCRIPTURE

READ 2 Peter 1:12–2:3 and 2 Peter 2:18-19. **MARK** every reference to *remind* including synonyms. Also **MARK** every reference to *prophecy*. **UNDERLINE** the tactics of the false teachers.

2 Peter 1:12–2:3

VOICES
Hearing God
in a World of
Impostors

New Testament

12 *Therefore, I will always be ready to remind you of these things, even though you already know them, and have been established in the truth which is present with you.*

13 *I consider it right, as long as I am in this earthly dwelling, to stir you up by way of reminder,*

14 *knowing that the laying aside of my earthly dwelling is imminent, as also our Lord Jesus Christ has made clear to me.*

15 *And I will also be diligent that at any time after my departure you will be able to call these things to mind.*

16 *For we did not follow cleverly devised tales when we made known to you the power and coming of our Lord Jesus Christ, but we were eyewitnesses of His majesty.*

17 *For when He received honor and glory from God the Father, such an utterance as this was made to Him by the Majestic Glory, "This is My beloved Son with whom I am well-pleased"—*

18 *and we ourselves heard this utterance made from heaven when we were with Him on the holy mountain.*

19 *So we have the prophetic word made more sure, to which you do well to pay attention as to a lamp shining in a dark place, until the day dawns and the morning star arises in your hearts.*

20 *But know this first of all, that no prophecy of Scripture is a matter of one's own interpretation,*

21 *for no prophecy was ever made by an act of human will, but men moved by the Holy Spirit spoke from God.*

1 *But false prophets also arose among the people, just as there will also be false teachers among you, who will secretly introduce destructive heresies, even denying the Master who bought them, bringing swift destruction upon themselves.*

2 *Many will follow their sensuality, and because of them the way of the truth will be maligned;*

3 *and in their greed they will exploit you with false words; their judgment from long ago is not idle, and their destruction is not asleep.*

2 Peter 2:18-19

18 *For speaking out arrogant words of vanity they entice by fleshly desires, by sensuality, those who barely escape from the ones who live in error,*

19 *promising them freedom while they themselves are slaves of corruption; for by what a man is overcome, by this he is enslaved.*

DISCUSS with your GROUP or PONDER on your own . . .

What is the focus of Peter's instruction? What does he want for his readers after he is gone? Why is this so important?

Why is Peter a reliable messenger?

What does he say about the prophecy? How does it happen? What does the Holy Spirit have to do with it?

If no prophecy ever came as an act of the human will, what does this tell you about those who humanly seek it out?

How does Peter describe false teachers? How will they operate? What will they teach? Who will they effect? Make a simple list of their characteristics.

How can you guard against false teachers? What specific steps can you take to protect your family and stand in your church?

OBSERVE the TEXT of SCRIPTURE

READ 2 Peter 3:1-2 and 13-18. Again, **MARK** every reference to *remind* including synonyms. Also **MARK** every command Peter makes and **UNDERLINE** the characteristics and tactics of unprincipled men.

2 Peter 3:1-2

1   *This is now, beloved, the second letter I am writing to you in which I am stirring up your sincere mind by way of reminder,*

2   *that you should remember the words spoken beforehand by the holy prophets and the commandment of the Lord and Savior spoken by your apostles.*

VOICES
Hearing God
in a World of
Impostors

New Testament

Week Five: **Empowered by the Spirit**

2 Peter 3:13-18

13 But according to His promise we are looking for new heavens and a new earth, in which righteousness dwells.

14 Therefore, beloved, since you look for these things, be diligent to be found by Him in peace, spotless and blameless,

15 and regard the patience of our Lord as salvation; just as also our beloved brother Paul, according to the wisdom given him, wrote to you,

16 as also in all his letters, speaking in them of these things, in which are some things hard to understand, which the untaught and unstable distort, as they do also the rest of the Scriptures, to their own destruction.

17 You therefore, beloved, knowing this beforehand, be on your guard so that you are not carried away by the error of unprincipled men and fall from your own steadfastness,

18 but grow in the grace and knowledge of our Lord and Savior Jesus Christ. To Him be the glory, both now and to the day of eternity. Amen.

DISCUSS with your GROUP or PONDER on your own . . .

What else does Peter remind his readers of? Whose writings does he call "scriptures"?

How does Peter describe the threats to the church?

How does Peter instruct his readers to live?

Which of his words will you begin or continue to apply this week?

@THE END OF THE DAY . . .

Take some time to consider how Peter's experiences compare with the instructions he gives to his readers. What is the focus of his exhortations? How are you doing at following God's commands through him?

Week Five: **Empowered by the Spirit**

VOICES
HEARING GOD
IN A WORLD OF
IMPOSTORS
New Testament

102

Paul: Obedient to the Heavenly Vision

"So, King Agrippa, I did not prove disobedient to the heavenly vision, but kept declaring both to those of Damascus first and also at Jerusalem and then throughout all the region of Judea, and even to the Gentiles, that they should repent and turn to God, performing deeds appropriate to repentance."
—Acts 26:19-20

Far from looking for a vision from God, Saul (aka Paul) was looking for Christians—chasing them, hunting them, seeking to kill them when Jesus hunted him down on the road to Damascus. Paul's life changed when he encountered the risen Christ and God put him on entirely new life path. As we did with Peter, let's look at both Paul's life experiences and his instruction to believers.

THE CONVERSION

Prior to his conversion, Paul was a Pharisee's Pharisee, a model Jewish man who followed the Law to the letter. He was present and complicit with the stoning of Stephen, the first Christian martyr in Acts 7, but God had other plans for him as Luke's account of Paul's conversion shows.

OBSERVE the TEXT of SCRIPTURE

READ Acts 9:1-20. **UNDERLINE** every phrase attributed to Jesus. Also **MARK** every reference to *Saul*.

Acts 9:1-20

1 *Now Saul, still breathing threats and murder against the disciples of the Lord, went to the high priest,*

2 *and asked for letters from him to the synagogues at Damascus, so that if he found any belonging to the Way, both men and women, he might bring them bound to Jerusalem.*

3 *As he was traveling, it happened that he was approaching Damascus, and suddenly a light from heaven flashed around him;*

4 *and he fell to the ground and heard a voice saying to him, "Saul, Saul, why are you persecuting Me?"*

5 *And he said, "Who are You, Lord?" And He said, "I am Jesus whom you are persecuting,*

6 *but get up and enter the city, and it will be told you what you must do."*

7 *The men who traveled with him stood speechless, hearing the voice but seeing no one.*

8 *Saul got up from the ground, and though his eyes were open, he could see nothing; and leading him by the hand, they brought him into Damascus.*

9 *And he was three days without sight, and neither ate nor drank.*

10 *Now there was a disciple at Damascus named Ananias; and the Lord said to him in a vision, "Ananias." And he said, "Here I am, Lord."*

11 *And the Lord said to him, "Get up and go to the street called Straight, and inquire at the house of Judas for a man from Tarsus named Saul, for he is praying,*

12 *and he has seen in a vision a man named Ananias come in and lay his hands on him, so that he might regain his sight."*

13 *But Ananias answered, "Lord, I have heard from many about this man, how much harm he did to Your saints at Jerusalem;*

14 *and here he has authority from the chief priests to bind all who call on Your name."*

15 *But the Lord said to him, "Go, for he is a chosen instrument of Mine, to bear My name before the Gentiles and kings and the sons of Israel;*

16 *for I will show him how much he must suffer for My name's sake."*

17 So Ananias departed and entered the house, and after laying his hands on him said, "Brother Saul, the Lord Jesus, who appeared to you on the road by which you were coming, has sent me so that you may regain your sight and be filled with the Holy Spirit."

18 And immediately there fell from his eyes something like scales, and he regained his sight, and he got up and was baptized;

19 and he took food and was strengthened.

Now for several days he was with the disciples who were at Damascus,

20 and immediately he began to proclaim Jesus in the synagogues, saying, "He is the Son of God."

DISCUSS with your GROUP or PONDER on your own . . .

Describe Saul and his pre-conversion mission.

What happens to him on the road to Damascus? What does he see and hear?

What does the voice ask him? Whose voice is it? What did He tell him to do?

What do Saul's traveling companions experience?

Describe Saul's condition after his encounter.

ONE STEP FURTHER:

Saul and/or Paul?

Why is the apostle referred to as "Saul" part of the time and "Paul" other times? If you have some time this week, see what you can find out about this name change. Observe when the shift occurs in the biblical text, then see what you can find out about the *Why?* of it. Consult your Bible dictionary and/or commentaries as appropriate and record your findings below.

ONE STEP FURTHER:

Word Study: Appeared

If you have some extra time, find the Greek word translated "appeared." See where else it is used with reference to Saul as well as how it is used elsewhere in the New Testament. Finally, note how what happens to Saul differs from what happens to his companions. Record your findings below.

VOICES
HEARING GOD
IN A WORLD OF
IMPOSTORS

Week Six: **Paul: Obedient to the Heavenly Vision**

Who is Ananias? What does the Lord tell him in a vision? List the specifics. How does it relate to Saul's vision?

How does Ananias respond to God's directives?

What does the Lord tell Ananias about Saul's future?

What does Saul begin doing after he is healed and filled with the Holy Spirit?

What confirms Saul's encounter with Jesus?

SETTING THE SCENE

Years later in front of Herod Agrippa, Paul recounts his conversion—or God's conversion of him—to Christianity.

OBSERVE the TEXT of SCRIPTURE

READ Acts 26:1-20 and **MARK** in a distinctive way every reference to *Paul* and every reference to *King Agrippa*. Remember to include pronouns.

Acts 26:1-20

1 Agrippa said to Paul, "You are permitted to speak for yourself." Then Paul stretched out his hand and proceeded to make his defense:

2 "In regard to all the things of which I am accused by the Jews, I consider myself fortunate, King Agrippa, that I am about to make my defense before you today;

3 especially because you are an expert in all customs and questions among the Jews; therefore I beg you to listen to me patiently.

4 "So then, all Jews know my manner of life from my youth up, which from the beginning was spent among my own nation and at Jerusalem;

5 since they have known about me for a long time, if they are willing to testify, that I lived as a Pharisee according to the strictest sect of our religion.

6 "And now I am standing trial for the hope of the promise made by God to our fathers;

7 the promise to which our twelve tribes hope to attain, as they earnestly serve God night and day. And for this hope, O King, I am being accused by Jews.

8 "Why is it considered incredible among you people if God does raise the dead?

9 "So then, I thought to myself that I had to do many things hostile to the name of Jesus of Nazareth.

10 "And this is just what I did in Jerusalem; not only did I lock up many of the saints in prisons, having received authority from the chief priests, but also when they were being put to death I cast my vote against them.

11 "And as I punished them often in all the synagogues, I tried to force them to blaspheme; and being furiously enraged at them, I kept pursuing them even to foreign cities.

12 "While so engaged as I was journeying to Damascus with the authority and commission of the chief priests,

13 at midday, O King, I saw on the way a light from heaven, brighter than the sun, shining all around me and those who were journeying with me.

14 "And when we had all fallen to the ground, I heard a voice saying to me in the Hebrew dialect, 'Saul, Saul, why are you persecuting Me? It is hard for you to kick against the goads.'

15 "And I said, 'Who are You, Lord?' And the Lord said, 'I am Jesus whom you are persecuting.

16 'But get up and stand on your feet; for this purpose I have appeared to you, to appoint you a minister and a witness not only to the things which you have seen, but also to the things in which I will appear to you;

17 rescuing you from the Jewish people and from the Gentiles, to whom I am sending you,

18 to open their eyes so that they may turn from darkness to light and from the dominion of Satan to God, that they may receive forgiveness of sins and an inheritance among those who have been sanctified by faith in Me.'

19 "So, King Agrippa, I did not prove disobedient to the heavenly vision,

20 but kept declaring both to those of Damascus first, and also at Jerusalem and then throughout all the region of Judea, and even to the Gentiles, that they should repent and turn to God, performing deeds appropriate to repentance.

FYI:

Three Ananias
From the Hebrew Hananiah, Ananias means "Yahweh has dealt graciously." In Acts, three men have the same name: lie-and-drop-dead Ananias (Acts 5), go-to-Saul Ananias (Acts 9), and high priest Ananias (Acts 23).

VOICES
HEARING GOD
IN A WORLD OF
IMPOSTORS

Week Six: **Paul: Obedient to the Heavenly Vision**

DISCUSS with your GROUP or PONDER on your own . . .

Under what circumstances is Paul telling about his conversion?

What does he tell about his life in Judaism? How had he acted toward the name of Jesus Christ and the saints?

What does he recount about his encounter with Jesus on the road to Damascus?

What additional information does he provide that is not recorded in Acts 9?

Why does Jesus say He appeared to Saul and how does Saul respond?

Do you know what God has called you to do? If so, what is it and how do you know?

Are you being obedient to the light you've been given?

What are some things we know from Scripture that are God's will for all believers?

How are you doing with these?

ONE STEP FURTHER:

God's Will

Paul recounts to Agrippa that Jesus told him He appeared to him for a specific reason: "for this purpose I have appeared to you, to appoint you a minister and a witness not only to the things which you have seen, but also to the things in which I will appear to you . . . (Acts 26:16). The purpose was a mission to turn people "from darkness to light and from the dominion of Satan to God" (Acts 26:18).

If you have time this week, search the Scriptures to find some purposes of God for all believers. What has God already revealed to be His will for His people? Record references to verses you already know, then run some word searches to help you uncover others. Start by searching "purpose," "will," and "desire" and see what you discover. Record your findings below.

VOICES
HEARING GOD
IN A WORLD OF
IMPOSTORS

108

New Testament

Digging Deeper

The Macedonian Vision

In Acts 16:6-10, God directs Paul by preventing him from going to two locations and giving him a vision of another. If you have some extra time this week, look into this passage for yourself and see what you can discover by further exploring some of the important words in the text.

Acts 16:6-10

6 *They passed through the Phrygian and Galatian region, having been forbidden by the Holy Spirit to speak the word in Asia;*

If you were to do a word study on one word of this verse, what would it be? Why? Where else is the word used? What does it mean?

7 *and after they came to Mysia, they were trying to go into Bithynia, and the Spirit of Jesus did not permit them;*

If you were to do a word study on one word of *this* verse, what would it be? Why? Where else is the word used? What does it mean?

8 *and passing by Mysia, they came down to Troas.*

9 *A vision appeared to Paul in the night: a man of Macedonia was standing and appealing to him, and saying, "Come over to Macedonia and help us."*

10 *When he had seen the vision, immediately we sought to go into Macedonia, concluding that God had called us to preach the gospel to them.*

What is the Greek word that is translated by "concluding"? Where else is it used in the New Testament? What did you learn about it?

Concisely explain the different elements God used to direct Paul to Macedonia.

FYI:

STOPPED! When God Blocks the Way

As adults it's easy for us to assume we have more power than we actually do—either for good or for harm. Acts 16 shows in no uncertain terms that God can and does stop people when He chooses to. Paul journeyed and spread the Gospel, "having been forbidden [*koluthentes*] by the Holy Spirit to speak the word in Asia." He also was not permitted (*ouk easen*) by the Spirit to go into Bithynia (Acts 16:6-7). While Paul wanted to spread the Gospel to Asia, he was not able to until the proper time on God's timetable. The same God who stopped Balaam (Numbers 22) and Jonah (Jonah 1–2) in their disobedience also kept Paul from moving forward in obedience until the time was right.

ONE STEP FURTHER:

Does the Word Get to Asia?

Yes! The Word gets to Asia through the Apostle Paul according to God's perfect time. If you have some extra time this week, see what you can discover about the specifics and record your findings below.

VOICES
HEARING GOD IN A WORLD OF IMPOSTORS

Week Six: **Paul: Obedient to the Heavenly Vision**

SETTING THE SCENE

In Paul's second letter to the Corinthians he is compelled to defend his apostleship. As part of this defense he refers to a revelatory vision he had.

OBSERVE the TEXT of SCRIPTURE

READ 2 Corinthians 12:1-12. **MARK** every occurrence of *boast* as well as any other key words you note. Observe the text carefully and we'll discuss it next week in class.

2 Corinthians 12:1-12

1   Boasting is necessary, though it is not profitable; but I will go on to visions and revelations of the Lord.

2   I know a man in Christ who fourteen years ago—whether in the body I do not know, or out of the body I do not know, God knows—such a man was caught up to the third heaven.

3   And I know how such a man—whether in the body or apart from the body I do not know, God knows—

4   was caught up into Paradise and heard inexpressible words, which a man is not permitted to speak.

5   On behalf of such a man I will boast; but on my own behalf I will not boast, except in regard to my weaknesses.

6   For if I do wish to boast I will not be foolish, for I will be speaking the truth; but I refrain from this, so that no one will credit me with more than he sees in me or hears from me.

7   Because of the surpassing greatness of the revelations, for this reason, to keep me from exalting myself, there was given me a thorn in the flesh, a messenger of Satan to torment me—to keep me from exalting myself!

8   Concerning this I implored the Lord three times that it might leave me.

9   And He has said to me, "My grace is sufficient for you, for power is perfected in weakness." Most gladly, therefore, I will rather boast about my weaknesses, so that the power of Christ may dwell in me.

10   Therefore I am well content with weaknesses, with insults, with distresses, with persecutions, with difficulties, for Christ's sake; for when I am weak, then I am strong.

11   I have become foolish; you yourselves compelled me. Actually I should have been commended by you, for in no respect was I inferior to the most eminent apostles, even though I am a nobody.

12   The signs of a true apostle were performed among you with all perseverance, by signs and wonders and miracles.

DISCUSS with your GROUP or PONDER on your own . . .

What does Paul bring up in verse 1?

ONE STEP FURTHER:

The Fortune-Telling Girl

While Paul and other apostles heard from God, other spirits were at work to deceive. If you have some time this week, look at the account of the fortune-telling slave girl in Acts 16:16-18. What power was at work in her? How was it working for her masters? How was it working against Paul? Describe her interaction with Paul. How does Paul view her and her message? What does he finally do? What does this tell us about the source? How does the Spirit at work in Paul differ from the spirit at work in the girl?

Who is Paul speaking about in 12:2-4? What did he experience? When did this happen?

What is the only thing Paul will boast in? Why?

What is Paul able to tell about this experience? What is he not allowed to tell?

What danger is he in because of "the surpassing greatness of the revelations"? What did God "give" Paul and for what reason?

What did Paul ask God to do about this torturous condition? How does God respond?

According to Paul, how should the Corinthians have treated him? Why?

In addition to the visions and revelations, what does Paul claim as signs of a true apostle?

Did "the signs of a true apostle" (2 Corinthians 12:12, Greek text literally: "the signs of the apostle") disappear with the Twelve Apostles? How were apostles defined (be sure to check 1 Corinthians 9:1)? Explain your answer from Scripture.

ONE STEP FURTHER:

Word Studies: Visions and Revelations

If you have time this week, find the Greek words translated by "visions" and "revelations." See how else they are used in Paul's writings and elsewhere in the New Testament. Record your findings below.

VOICES
HEARING GOD
IN A WORLD OF
IMPOSTORS

NOTES

Mid-Week Wrap-Up . . .

Do you have any remaining questions from this week? If so, what are they? What has been your biggest takeaway application?

THE PASTORALS: Titus, 1 and 2 Timothy

In our day and age, existentialism reigns. Nothing can challenge feelings in the marketplace of ideas where "what it means to me" consistently trumps "what it means." When Paul wrote his pastoral epistles, however, he stressed to his young protégés the importance of a standard by which everything else could be measured and compared.

OBSERVE the TEXT of SCRIPTURE

READ the incredibly short book of Titus—three chapters, no big thing! Then **RE-READ**, Titus 1 and **MARK** every reference to *sound* and every reference to the *word*.

Titus 1

1   *Paul, a bond-servant of God and an apostle of Jesus Christ, for the faith of those chosen of God and the knowledge of the truth which is according to godliness,*

2   *in the hope of eternal life, which God, who cannot lie, promised long ages ago,*

3   *but at the proper time manifested, even His word, in the proclamation with which I was entrusted according to the commandment of God our Savior,*

4   *To Titus, my true child in a common faith: Grace and peace from God the Father and Christ Jesus our Savior.*

5   *For this reason I left you in Crete, that you would set in order what remains and appoint elders in every city as I directed you,*

6   *namely, if any man is above reproach, the husband of one wife, having children who believe, not accused of dissipation or rebellion.*

7   *For the overseer must be above reproach as God's steward, not self-willed, not quick-tempered, not addicted to wine, not pugnacious, not fond of sordid gain,*

8   *but hospitable, loving what is good, sensible, just, devout, self-controlled,*

9   *holding fast the faithful word which is in accordance with the teaching, so that he will be able both to exhort in sound doctrine and to refute those who contradict.*

10 *For there are many rebellious men, empty talkers and deceivers, especially those of the circumcision,*

11 *who must be silenced because they are upsetting whole families, teaching things they should not teach for the sake of sordid gain.*

12 *One of themselves, a prophet of their own, said, "Cretans are always liars, evil beasts, lazy gluttons."*

13 *This testimony is true. For this reason reprove them severely so that they may be sound in the faith,*

14 *not paying attention to Jewish myths and commandments of men who turn away from the truth.*

15 *To the pure, all things are pure; but to those who are defiled and unbelieving, nothing is pure, but both their mind and their conscience are defiled.*

16 *They profess to know God, but by their deeds they deny Him, being detestable and disobedient and worthless for any good deed.*

DISCUSS with your GROUP or PONDER on your own . . .

Paul tells Titus to appoint elders. What are the elders to do with regard to the Word? How are they to exhort?

Paul says they are to refute those who contradict. Is there a standard they can use to determine what contradicts? If so, what is it?

Have you observed contentions over disparate views among believers being addressed? Were they addressed biblically? Explain.

According to Paul, what is the standard? Where does "the burden of proof" lie? How does this fit with current "sensibilities"? Explain your thoughts.

Week Six: **Paul: Obedient to the Heavenly Vision**

How does Paul describe rebellious men? What characterizes them? What is their relationship to the truth?

According to verse 16, how can we tell the difference between someone who truly knows God and someone who only professes to know Him?

Is this immediately recognizable? Explain your answer and support it biblically.

FYI:

What is Doctrine?

Simply put, doctrine is something that is taught. The Greek word *didaskalia*—translated "doctrine" four times in the book of Titus—is from the Greek *didasko* which means "to teach." Of its twenty-one appearances in the New Testament, fifteen appear in the Pastoral Epistles of 1 and 2 Timothy and Titus translated either "doctrine" or "teaching."

RE-READ, Titus 2 and **MARK** every reference to *doctrine* and every reference to the *sensible*.

Titus 2

1   But as for you, speak the things which are fitting for sound doctrine.

2   Older men are to be temperate, dignified, sensible, sound in faith, in love, in perseverance.

3   Older women likewise are to be reverent in their behavior, not malicious gossips nor enslaved to much wine, teaching what is good,

4   so that they may encourage the young women to love their husbands, to love their children,

5   to be sensible, pure, workers at home, kind, being subject to their own husbands, so that the word of God will not be dishonored.

6   Likewise urge the young men to be sensible;

7   in all things show yourself to be an example of good deeds, with purity in doctrine, dignified,

8   sound in speech which is beyond reproach, so that the opponent will be put to shame, having nothing bad to say about us.

9   Urge bondslaves to be subject to their own masters in everything, to be well-pleasing, not argumentative,

10 not pilfering, but showing all good faith so that they will adorn the doctrine of God our Savior in every respect.

11 For the grace of God has appeared, bringing salvation to all men,

12 instructing us to deny ungodliness and worldly desires and to live sensibly, righteously and godly in the present age,

13 looking for the blessed hope and the appearing of the glory of our great God and Savior, Christ Jesus,

14 who gave Himself for us to redeem us from every lawless deed, and to purify for Himself a people for His own possession, zealous for good deeds.

15 These things speak and exhort and reprove with all authority. Let no one disregard you.

DISCUSS with your GROUP or PONDER on your own . . .

What does Paul say about doctrine in Titus 2? What characterizes it?

How are we to live in the light of the doctrine of God our Savior?

Who is told to be sensible and live sensibly? Why?

What instructions are laid out in verses 12-13?

What are we to look for?

How are you doing at adorning the doctrine of God our Savior?

RE-READ Titus 3 and **UNDERLINE** all of Paul's instructions to Titus (you're looking for imperative verbs).

Titus 3

1 Remind them to be subject to rulers, to authorities, to be obedient, to be ready for every good deed,

---

ONE STEP FURTHER:

Word Study: Sensible

If you have extra time this week, find the Greek word translated by "sensible." How many times does a form of the word show up in Titus 2? Where else does Paul use it? Where else is it used in the New Testament and how is it used? Record your findings below.

ONE STEP FURTHER:

The Appearing

Paul tells Titus that the grace of God disciplines (*paideuo*) believers to look for the appearing (singular) of our great God and Savior, Christ Jesus. How does this compare with what people are looking for today? What do you look for regularly?

ONE STEP FURTHER:

Factious

The Greek adjective translated "factious" appears only in Titus 3:10 in the New Testament. But the root noun (*airesis*) and verb (*aireo*) that are related to this one-off adjective appears frequently. It's an interesting Greek word that may surprise you. See what you can discover about its root and cognates (associated words: nouns and verbs) and what English words typically translate them.

2 to malign no one, to be peaceable, gentle, showing every consideration for all men.

3 For we also once were foolish ourselves, disobedient, deceived, enslaved to various lusts and pleasures, spending our life in malice and envy, hateful, hating one another.

4 But when the kindness of God our Savior and His love for mankind appeared,

5 He saved us, not on the basis of deeds which we have done in righteousness, but according to His mercy, by the washing of regeneration and renewing by the Holy Spirit,

6 whom He poured out upon us richly through Jesus Christ our Savior,

7 so that being justified by His grace we would be made heirs according to the hope of eternal life.

8 This is a trustworthy statement; and concerning these things I want you to speak confidently, so that those who have believed God will be careful to engage in good deeds. These things are good and profitable for men.

9 But avoid foolish controversies and genealogies and strife and disputes about the Law, for they are unprofitable and worthless.

10 Reject a factious man after a first and second warning,

11 knowing that such a man is perverted and is sinning, being self-condemned.

12 When I send Artemas or Tychicus to you, make every effort to come to me at Nicopolis, for I have decided to spend the winter there.

13 Diligently help Zenas the lawyer and Apollos on their way so that nothing is lacking for them.

14 Our people must also learn to engage in good deeds to meet pressing needs, so that they will not be unfruitful.

15 All who are with me greet you. Greet those who love us in the faith. Grace be with you all.

DISCUSS with your GROUP or PONDER on your own . . .

In Titus 3, what does Paul tell Titus to do?

How does He describe salvation with respect to the Holy Spirit? How does this compare with what we examined in Acts with reference to the baptism of the Holy Spirit?

VOICES
HEARING GOD
IN A WORLD OF
IMPOSTORS

116

New Testament

What does he tell Titus to avoid and reject? Why?

Looking back at the whole of Titus, where does Paul point Titus for truth? Does he point anywhere else? Cite your answers.

Based on Paul's letter to Titus, where should disciples look for truth?

Digging Deeper

1 Timothy and 2 Timothy

If you have time this week, read 1 Timothy and 2 Timothy in their entireties and work through the questions below.

What does Paul exhort Timothy to do and instruct him to learn?

According to Paul, where do we seek truth?

Does he ever say to seek it in other places?

Summarize Paul's message to Timothy.

ONE STEP FURTHER:

Foolish controversy or hill to die on?

Paul clearly tells Titus both to exhort in sound doctrine and to avoid foolish controversies. In Christian culture today, what issues would you categorize as doctrinal and which would you categorize as foolish controversies? Think it through and record some examples of both below along with reasoning to support your views.

Doctrinal Issues

Foolish Controversies

OBSERVE the TEXT of SCRIPTURE

READ 1 Timothy 1:1-11. **MARK** every reference to *teaching* and *instruction*.

1 Timothy 1:1-11

1 *Paul, an apostle of Christ Jesus according to the commandment of God our Savior, and of Christ Jesus,* who is *our hope,*

2 *To Timothy,* my *true child in the* faith: *Grace, mercy and peace from God the Father and Christ Jesus our Lord.*

3 *As I urged you upon my departure for Macedonia, remain on at Ephesus so that you may instruct certain men not to teach strange doctrines,*

4 *nor to pay attention to myths and endless genealogies, which give rise to mere speculation rather than furthering the administration of God which is by faith.*

5 *But the goal of our instruction is love from a pure heart and a good conscience and a sincere faith.*

6 *For some men, straying from these things, have turned aside to fruitless discussion,*

7 *wanting to be teachers of the Law, even though they do not understand either what they are saying or the matters about which they make confident assertions.*

8 *But we know that the Law is good, if one uses it lawfully,*

9 *realizing the fact that law is not made for a righteous person, but for those who are lawless and rebellious, for the ungodly and sinners, for the unholy and profane, for those who kill their fathers or mothers, for murderers*

10 *and immoral men and homosexuals and kidnappers and liars and perjurers, and whatever else is contrary to sound teaching,*

11 *according to the glorious gospel of the blessed God, with which I have been entrusted.*

DISCUSS with your GROUP or PONDER on your own . . .

What does Paul warn against? What do these kinds of behavior and thinking produce?

By contrast, what is Paul's goal in instruction? What does his teaching produce?

According to verses 10-11, what standard does Paul use for comparison?

Have you seen the contrast between strange and sound doctrines up close and personal? If so, were you able to discern it by using the Word as a plumbline? Explain.

OBSERVE the TEXT of SCRIPTURE

READ 1 Timothy 4:1-8. **MARK** in a distinctive way the references to *sound doctrine* versus *demonic doctrines*.

I Timothy 4:1-8

1 *But the Spirit explicitly says that in later times some will fall away from the faith, paying attention to deceitful spirits and doctrines of demons,*

2 *by means of the hypocrisy of liars seared in their own conscience as with a branding iron,*

3 *men who forbid marriage and advocate abstaining from foods which God has created to be gratefully shared in by those who believe and know the truth.*

4 *For everything created by God is good, and nothing is to be rejected if it is received with gratitude;*

5 *for it is sanctified by means of the word of God and prayer.*

6 *In pointing out these things to the brethren, you will be a good servant of Christ Jesus, constantly nourished on the words of the faith and of the sound doctrine which you have been following.*

7 *But have nothing to do with worldly fables fit only for old women. On the other hand, discipline yourself for the purpose of godliness;*

8 *for bodily discipline is only of little profit, but godliness is profitable for all things, since it holds promise for the present life and also for the life to come.*

> **FYI:**
>
> **Read the Book**
> *Until I come, give attention to the public reading of Scripture, to exhortation and teaching.*
> —1 Timothy 4:13, NASB

DISCUSS with your GROUP or PONDER on your own . . .

According to Paul, what does the Spirit "explicitly say" will happen in later times?

VOICES
Hearing God
in a World of
Impostors

Week Six: **Paul: Obedient to the Heavenly Vision**

What other doctrines does Paul warn about? Where do they originate? What behaviors will they generate compared to those of sound doctrine?

Doctrines of Demons	versus	Sound Doctrine

How can Christ's servants stand in the face of this? What are we to do and not to do?

How are you doing at these?

OBSERVE the TEXT of SCRIPTURE

READ 1 Timothy 6:20-21. **UNDERLINE** what Timothy is to avoid.

I Timothy 6:20-21

20 *O Timothy, guard what has been entrusted to you, avoiding worldly and empty chatter and the opposing arguments of what is falsely called "knowledge"—*

21 *which some have professed and thus gone astray from the faith. Grace be with you.*

DISCUSS with your GROUP or PONDER on your own . . .

What is it that Timothy is to guard? What has been entrusted to him? (Read more context if you need to!)

Does everyone who claims to have knowledge actually have knowledge? What has happened to some who have claimed knowledge?

Are you guarding what has been entrusted to you? If so, how?

Are you engaging or avoiding false forms of speech—worldly and empty chatter and opposing arguments of what is falsely called "knowledge"? Explain.

Again, what does Paul point Timothy to for truth? Does he point to any other places? Where do you go for truth? Why?

OBSERVE the TEXT of SCRIPTURE

READ the following verses from 2 Timothy, Paul's final written words prior to his death at the hands of Rome. **UNDERLINE** Paul's instructions to Timothy.

2 Timothy 1:13-14

13 Retain the standard of sound words which you have heard from me, in the faith and love which are in Christ Jesus.

14 Guard, through the Holy Spirit who dwells in us, the treasure which has been entrusted to you.

2 Timothy 2:1-2

1 You therefore, my son, be strong in the grace that is in Christ Jesus.

2 The things which you have heard from me in the presence of many witnesses, entrust these to faithful men who will be able to teach others also.

2 Timothy 2:14-15

14 Remind them of these things, and solemnly charge them in the presence of God not to wrangle about words, which is useless and leads to the ruin of the hearers.

15 Be diligent to present yourself approved to God as a workman who does not need to be ashamed, accurately handling the word of truth.

VOICES
Hearing God
in a World of
Impostors

New Testament

121

Week Six: **Paul: Obedient to the Heavenly Vision**

2 Timothy 3:14-17

14 *You, however, continue in the things you have learned and become convinced of, knowing from whom you have learned them,*

15 *and that from childhood you have known the sacred writings which are able to give you the wisdom that leads to salvation through faith which is in Christ Jesus.*

16 *All Scripture is inspired by God and profitable for teaching, for reproof, for correction, for training in righteousness;*

17 *so that the man of God may be adequate, equipped for every good work.*

2 Timothy 4:1-5

1 *I solemnly charge you in the presence of God and of Christ Jesus, who is to judge the living and the dead, and by His appearing and His kingdom:*

2 *preach the word; be ready in season and out of season; reprove, rebuke, exhort, with great patience and instruction.*

3 *For the time will come when they will not endure sound doctrine; but wanting to have their ears tickled, they will accumulate for themselves teachers in accordance to their own desires,*

4 *and will turn away their ears from the truth and will turn aside to myths.*

5 *But you, be sober in all things, endure hardship, do the work of an evangelist, fulfill your ministry.*

DISCUSS with your GROUP or PONDER on your own . . .

What instructions does Paul give Timothy in these verses?

What does he specifically say about the Word?

How is Timothy to teach and encourage others?

What threats will come to sound doctrine and how is Timothy to respond?

How are you doing at properly handling and passing on the word of truth?

@THE END OF THE DAY . . .

Take some time to look back through this week's lesson and compare Paul's visions to his teaching. What does he recount about the visions he was given? Think specifically of purposes and results. Then compare these with the specific instructions he gives to the next generation to pursue. Where does Paul primarily point people in order to hear the true voice of God and pick out impostors? Record your thoughts below.

Week Six: **Paul: Obedient to the Heavenly Vision**

VOICES
HEARING GOD
IN A WORLD OF
IMPOSTORS
New Testament

124

Paul: Walking by the Spirit

But if anyone does not have the Spirit of Christ,
he does not belong to Him.
—Romans 8:9b

While Paul had revelations, performed miracles and saw visions, his life was characterized by walking by the Spirit. Even though Jesus appeared to him on the road to Damascus, Paul's normal Christian life was one of walking by the Spirit, not always knowing what the next step would be or what the right answer to a specific issue was. Consider for a moment his clash with Barnabas over Mark's "credentials" for ministry. Paul took his opinion and Silas to Syria and Cilicia while Barnabas took Mark and went to Cyprus. No casting lots, no "Thus says the Lord." All the men continued in ministry and at the end of his life Paul referred to Mark as 'useful" (2 Timothy 4:11).

Walking by the Spirit is not confusing, but the Spirit does not give us heads-or-tails clarity to all issues and problems we confront. Remember, as we learned, the Spirit does not speak on His own; He takes Jesus' words (the Word of God) and repeats them to us. The Spirit leads us to all (and only) truth, but God does not reveal all truth He knows. Since the Spirit is the truth (1 John 5:6), to walk by the Spirit is to walk by the Truth God has revealed to us in His Word. We have God's Word and we have God's Spirit who leads us to this revealed truth. Let s take a look together at some of the highlights of Paul's teaching on walking by the Spirit and his warnings about impostors who seek to deceive.

WALKING BY THE SPIRIT: ROMANS

Perhaps the most developed biblical exposition of being led by the Spirit appears in Romans 8. In context, Paul has been laying out the Gospel message of sin, salvation, and sanctification which happens by God's sovereignty for God's service. Romans 8 is the heart of his teaching on sanctification—being made holy and living out the reality of the change within us by the power of the indwelling Spirit.

OBSERVE the TEXT of SCRIPTURE

READ Romans 8 and **MARK** every reference to the *Spirit*. Then, **MARK** every reference to the *mind* or *mind set*.

Romans 8

1   Therefore there is now no condemnation for those who are in Christ Jesus.

2   For the law of the Spirit of life in Christ Jesus has set you free from the law of sin and of death.

3   For what the Law could not do, weak as it was through the flesh, God did: sending His own Son in the likeness of sinful flesh and as an offering *for sin*, He condemned sin in the flesh,

4   so that the requirement of the Law might be fulfilled in us, who do not walk according to the flesh but according to the Spirit.

5   For those who are according to the flesh set their minds on the things of the flesh, but those who are according to the Spirit, the things of the Spirit.

6   For the mind set on the flesh is death, but the mind set on the Spirit is life and peace,

7   because the mind set on the flesh is hostile toward God; for it does not subject itself to the law of God, for it is not even able to do so,

8   and those who are in the flesh cannot please God.

9   However, you are not in the flesh but in the Spirit, if indeed the Spirit of God dwells in you. But if anyone does not have the Spirit of Christ, he does not belong to Him.

10   If Christ is in you, though the body is dead because of sin, yet the spirit is alive because of righteousness.

11   But if the Spirit of Him who raised Jesus from the dead dwells in you, He who raised Christ Jesus from the dead will also give life to your mortal bodies through His Spirit who dwells in you.

12   So then, brethren, we are under obligation, not to the flesh, to live according to the flesh—

13   for if you are living according to the flesh, you must die; but if by the Spirit you are putting to death the deeds of the body, you will live.

14   For all who are being led by the Spirit of God, these are sons of God.

15   For you have not received a spirit of slavery leading to fear again, but you have received a spirit of adoption as sons by which we cry out, "Abba! Father!"

ONE STEP FURTHER:

Word Study: Mind Set

This week, find the Greek noun that is translated by "mind set" (note: a noun and a verb). Where else is it used? (Don't miss it in Romans 12!) How is it used? Record your findings below.

VOICES
HEARING GOD
IN A WORLD OF
IMPOSTORS

126

New Testament

16 *The Spirit Himself testifies with our spirit that we are children of God,*

17 *and if children, heirs also, heirs of God and fellow heirs with Christ, if indeed we suffer with Him so that we may also be glorified with Him.*

18 *For I consider that the sufferings of this present time are not worthy to be compared with the glory that is to be revealed to us.*

19 *For the anxious longing of the creation waits eagerly for the revealing of the sons of God.*

20 *For the creation was subjected to futility, not willingly, but because of Him who subjected it, in hope*

21 *that the creation itself also will be set free from its slavery to corruption into the freedom of the glory of the children of God.*

22 *For we know that the whole creation groans and suffers the pains of childbirth together until now.*

23 *And not only this, but also we ourselves, having the first fruits of the Spirit, even we ourselves groan within ourselves, waiting eagerly for our adoption as sons, the redemption of our body.*

24 *For in hope we have been saved, but hope that is seen is not hope; for who hopes for what he already sees?*

25 *But if we hope for what we do not see, with perseverance we wait eagerly for it.*

26 *In the same way the Spirit also helps our weakness; for we do not know how to pray as we should, but the Spirit Himself intercedes for us with groanings too deep for words;*

27 *and He who searches the hearts knows what the mind of the Spirit is, because He intercedes for the saints according to the will of God.*

28 *And we know that God causes all things to work together for good to those who love God, to those who are called according to His purpose.*

29 *For those whom He foreknew, He also predestined to become conformed to the image of His Son, so that He would be the firstborn among many brethren;*

30 *and these whom He predestined, He also called; and these whom He called, He also justified; and these whom He justified, He also glorified.*

31 *What then shall we say to these things? If God is for us, who is against us?*

32 *He who did not spare His own Son, but delivered Him over for us all, how will He not also with Him freely give us all things?*

33 *Who will bring a charge against God's elect? God is the one who justifies;*

34 *who is the one who condemns? Christ Jesus is He who died, yes, rather who was raised, who is at the right hand of God, who also intercedes for us.*

35 *Who will separate us from the love of Christ? Will tribulation, or distress, or persecution, or famine, or nakedness, or peril, or sword?*

36 *Just as it is written,*

"FOR YOUR SAKE WE ARE BEING PUT TO DEATH ALL DAY LONG;

ONE STEP FURTHER:

Word Study: Led
What is the Greek word for "led" in Romans 8:14? See what you can learn about it this week.

ONE STEP FURTHER:

Word Study: Waits Eagerly
Locate the Greek word and investigate where else it is used in the New Testament and how. Record your findings below.

VOICES
HEARING GOD IN A WORLD OF IMPOSTORS

New Testament 127

WE WERE CONSIDERED AS SHEEP TO BE SLAUGHTERED."

37 *But in all these things we overwhelmingly conquer through Him who loved us.*

38 *For I am convinced that neither death, nor life, nor angels, nor principalities, nor things present, nor things to come, nor powers,*

39 *nor height, nor depth, nor any other created thing, will be able to separate us from the love of God, which is in Christ Jesus our Lord.*

ONE STEP FURTHER:

Word Study: Hope

If you have some more time, also find the Greek root word for "hope." Counting both noun and verb forms, the root appears six times in Romans 8:20-25 alone. Note how it is used throughout Romans, elsewhere in Paul's writings and in the rest of the New Testament. Record your findings below.

DISCUSS with your GROUP or PONDER on your own (Romans 8:1-17) . . .

Taking note of where you marked "Spirit," compile a list of everything Paul teaches about the Spirit in Romans 8:1-17.

What will those who are "according the Spirit" avoid and what will they *not* get?

How do we practically "walk according to the Spirit"? What are examples of the mind set on the Spirit? What thought does this involve? What actions follow?

What characterizes the mind set on the flesh?

Compare the mind set on the flesh with the mind set on the Spirit. Give an example of each.

How critical is it to have the Spirit? Explain.

How does Paul define "sons of God"? How do "sons" know they are children of God? Do you know that you are a child of God? Explain.

VOICES
HEARING GOD
IN A WORLD OF
IMPOSTORS

128

New Testament

NOTES

DISCUSS with your GROUP or PONDER on your own (Romans 8:18-30) . . .

First, **RE-READ** Romans 8:18-30 and **MARK** every reference to *waits eagerly*. Then **MARK** every reference to *hope(s)*.

What and/or who is "eagerly waiting" and for what?

What does Paul say about hope in verses 24-25?

What judgments have been placed on creation according to verses 18-24? Are children of God affected by these? How?

Is there any doubt about the salvation of God's children? What happens now and what happens later and when?

How does the Spirit help our weaknesses according to verses 26-27?

If there are times when we don't even know how to pray, does it stand to reason that there are times when we don't know how to act (beyond obvious general categories like honoring God and others above self, etc.)? Explain your answer.

What does Paul say we know according to verse 28?

How can this truth bring comfort and assurance in times when you "don't know" other things?

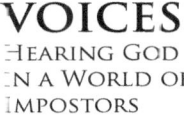

VOICES
HEARING GOD
IN A WORLD OF
IMPOSTORS

Week Seven: **Paul: Walking by the Spirit**

DISCUSS with your GROUP or PONDER on your own (Romans 8:31-38) . . .

First, **RE-READ** Romans 8:31-38 and **MARK** every reference to *love*. Then **MARK** every reference anything negative or harmful.

What does Paul say about God's love for us in Christ in this section? How did He demonstrate His love?

What threats does Paul mention?

What does walking by the Spirit have to do with facing the obstacles Paul describes?

What is the main message of this section of the text? What assurance does this give you?

How would you describe life in the Spirit on the basis of Romans 8?

SETTING THE SCENE

In Romans 12 Paul moves from doctrinal teaching about the Gospel, to application. Based on what God has done, what are His people to do in response? Let's look.

OBSERVE the TEXT of SCRIPTURE

READ Romans 12:1-3. **MARK** every reference the *mind*, *thinking*, and *judgment*.

Romans 12:1-3

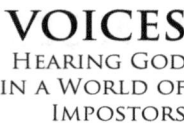

1 Therefore I urge you, brethren, by the mercies of God, to present your bodies a living and holy sacrifice, acceptable to God, which is *your spiritual service of worship.*

2 And do not be conformed to this world, but be transformed by the renewing of your mind, so that you may prove what the will of God is, that which is good and acceptable and perfect.

3 For through the grace given to me I say to everyone among you not to think more highly of himself than he ought to think; but to think so as to have sound judgment, as God has allotted to each a measure of faith.

DISCUSS with your GROUP or PONDER on your own . . .

What does Paul urge his readers to do in verse 1?

What does he command them to do and not do in verse 2?

How can they obey? What actions can they take? What will this involve?

What should characterize the Christian mind and thinking?

Do you think with sound judgment or are you tossed about by feelings? Explain.

WALKING BY THE SPIRIT: CORINTHIANS

Unlike Romans which was written to a church Paul had yet to visit, the Corinthian letters were written to a church that Paul had been involved in planting.

FYI:

Preaching the Gospel

While God could have chosen to bring people to Himself through visions and dreams if He had wanted, Scripture indicates that He chose to speak the Good News of Jesus through the preaching of the Word (Heb 1:1, 2; Acts 10:36). Consider Paul's words from Romans 10:12-17:

12 For there is no distinction between Jew and Greek; for the same Lord is Lord of all, abounding in riches for all who call on Him;

13 for "WHOEVER WILL CALL ON THE NAME OF THE LORD WILL BE SAVED."

14 How then will they call on Him in whom they have not believed? How will they believe in Him whom they have not heard? And how will they hear without a preacher?

15 How will they preach unless they are sent? Just as it is written, "HOW BEAUTIFUL ARE THE FEET OF THOSE WHO BRING GOOD NEWS OF GOOD THINGS!"

16 However, they did not all heed the good news; for Isaiah says, "LORD, WHO HAS BELIEVED OUR REPORT?"

17 So faith comes from hearing, and hearing by the word of Christ.

Is it possible that Muslims are converting based on dreams and visions in which they hear the word of Christ? Evidence suggests this is happening around the world consistent with the prophecy of Joel 2:28-29 and Acts 2:14-21. Perhaps it is also an additional fulfillment of Genesis 17:20.

VOICES
HEARING GOD
IN A WORLD OF
IMPOSTORS

OBSERVE the TEXT of SCRIPTURE

READ 1 Corinthians 2. **MARK** in a unique way every occurrence of *wisdom*, of *Spirit*, and of *appraises*.

1 Corinthians 2

1 *And when I came to you, brethren, I did not come with superiority of speech or of wisdom, proclaiming to you the testimony of God.*

2 *For I determined to know nothing among you except Jesus Christ, and Him crucified.*

3 *I was with you in weakness and in fear and in much trembling,*

4 *and my message and my preaching were not in persuasive words of wisdom, but in demonstration of the Spirit and of power,*

5 *so that your faith would not rest on the wisdom of men, but on the power of God.*

6 *Yet we do speak wisdom among those who are mature; a wisdom, however, not of this age nor of the rulers of this age, who are passing away;*

7 *but we speak God's wisdom in a mystery, the hidden wisdom which God predestined before the ages to our glory;*

8 *the wisdom which none of the rulers of this age has understood; for if they had understood it they would not have crucified the Lord of glory;*

9 *but just as it is written,*

"THINGS WHICH EYE HAS NOT SEEN AND EAR HAS NOT HEARD,

AND which HAVE NOT ENTERED THE HEART OF MAN,

ALL THAT GOD HAS PREPARED FOR THOSE WHO LOVE HIM."

10 *For to us God revealed them through the Spirit; for the Spirit searches all things, even the depths of God.*

11 *For who among men knows the thoughts of a man except the spirit of the man which is in him? Even so the thoughts of God no one knows except the Spirit of God.*

12 *Now we have received, not the spirit of the world, but the Spirit who is from God, so that we may know the things freely given to us by God,*

13 *which things we also speak, not in words taught by human wisdom, but in those taught by the Spirit, combining spiritual thoughts with spiritual words.*

14 *But a natural man does not accept the things of the Spirit of God, for they are foolishness to him; and he cannot understand them, because they are spiritually appraised.*

15 *But he who is spiritual appraises all things, yet he himself is appraised by no one.*

16 *For WHO HAS KNOWN THE MIND OF THE LORD, THAT HE WILL INSTRUCT HIM? But we have the mind of Christ.*

FYI:

Crucified with Christ

In one of the most concise verses on living the Christian life, Paul summarizes our life as Christ living in us. We have been united to His death at the cross and are united to His life here and now, on this planet, in our spirits.

"I have been crucified with Christ; and it is no longer I who live, but Christ lives in me; and the life which I now live in the flesh I live by faith in the Son of God, who loved me and gave Himself up for me."

–Galatians 2:20

DISCUSS with your GROUP or PONDER on your own . . .

How does Paul describe his preaching? What is primary content of his preaching?

What does he want the Corinthians' faith to rest on?

What wisdom types does Paul contrast?

Who does Paul say knows the thoughts of God? How does this relate to our knowing God?

What does Paul say we *will* know in verse 12? Does this include everything? Explain.

Can we expect God to reveal all things to us? Defend your answer from Scripture.

Why are things of the Spirit not understood by the natural man?

What does "spiritually appraised" mean? As you answer, consider the voices (active or passive) of the verbs in verses 14 and 15.

What do those who are spiritual appraise? How are you doing at this?

PAUL'S PRAYERS:

As we continue to look at Paul's letters, let's turn our attention to some of his prayers for his readers and then to instructions and warnings.

OBSERVE the TEXT of SCRIPTURE

READ Ephesians 1:15-23. **UNDERLINE** everything Paul asks God to give to the Ephesian believers.

Ephesians 1:15-23

15 *For this reason I too, having heard of the faith in the Lord Jesus which* exists *among you and your love for all the saints,*

16 *do not cease giving thanks for you, while making mention* of you *in my prayers;*

Digging Deeper

Galatians

If you have time this week, read through Galatians paying close attention to Paul's descriptions of revelations he had and to his instruction about walking by the Spirit.

What revelations does Paul talk about? What was the purpose of each?

Galatians 1:12

Galatians 2:2

What does Paul say about walking by the Spirit in Galatians 5:13-26?

ONE STEP FURTHER:

Word Study: Appraise

If you have time this week, find the Greek word translated by "appraise." Does the text define it? Does its use elsewhere in the New Testament help us? Record your findings below.

17 that the God of our Lord Jesus Christ, the Father of glory, may give to you a *spirit of wisdom and of revelation in the knowledge of Him.*

18 I pray that *the eyes of your heart may be enlightened, so that you will know what is the hope of His calling, what are the riches of the glory of His inheritance in the saints,*

19 and what is the surpassing greatness of His power toward us who believe. These are *in accordance with the working of the strength of His might*

20 which He brought about in Christ, when He raised Him from the dead and seated Him at His right hand in the heavenly col

21 far above all rule and authority and power and dominion, and every name that is named, not only in this age but also in the one to come.

22 And He put all things in subjection under His feet, and gave Him as head over all things to the church,

23 which is His body, the fullness of Him who fills all in all.

FYI:

The Secret Things

"The secret things belong to the LORD our God, but the things revealed belong to us and to our sons forever, that we may observe all the words of this law."

—Deuteronomy 29:29

DISCUSS with your GROUP or PONDER on your own . . .

What is the spiritual condition of the people Paul is praying for? What does he ask God for on their behalf? What does he pray that they will know?

What did we learn about hope in Romans 8? Is hope visible? Why/why not?

What kind of power is toward us who believe? What difference does this make in our lives?

OBSERVE the TEXT of SCRIPTURE

READ Colossians 1:9-12 and **UNDERLINE** everything Paul prays for the Colossians. Then **MARK** every occurrence of *all* and *every* (Greek *pas*).

Colossians 1:9-12

9 *For this reason also, since the day we heard of it, we have not ceased to pray for you and to ask that you may be filled with the knowledge of His will in all spiritual wisdom and understanding,*

Week Seven: **Paul: Walking by the Spirit**

10 so that you will walk in a manner worthy of the Lord, to please Him *in all respects*, bearing fruit in every good work and increasing in the knowledge of God;

11 strengthened with all power, according to His glorious might, for the attaining of all steadfastness and patience; joyously

12 giving thanks to the Father, who has qualified us to share in the inheritance of the saints in Light.

DISCUSS with your GROUP or PONDER on your own . . .

What does Paul pray for the Colossians? How does this compare with his prayer for the Ephesian church?

What is the purpose of his prayer? How complete or thorough is his request? Explain.

Have you ever prayed this for someone before? Can you think of someone you might want to pray this for regularly?

INSTRUCTIONS and WARNINGS

Throughout his letters to the churches, Paul warns Christ's followers to beware of threats to the faith.

SETTING THE SCENE

Paul has just talked about building the body to maturity through proper use of spiritual gifts.

OBSERVE the TEXT of SCRIPTURE

READ Ephesians 4:14-24 **MARK** every reference to *growing up*, including synonyms.

VOICES
HEARING GOD
IN A WORLD OF
IMPOSTORS

136

New Testament

Ephesians 4:14-24

14 As a result, we are no longer to be children, tossed here and there by waves and carried about by every wind of doctrine, by the trickery of men, by craftiness in deceitful scheming;

15 but speaking the truth in love, we are to grow up in all aspects into Him who is the head, even Christ,

16 from whom the whole body, being fitted and held together by what every joint supplies, according to the proper working of each individual part, causes the growth of the body for the building up of itself in love.

17 So this I say, and affirm together with the Lord, that you walk no longer just as the Gentiles also walk, in the futility of their mind,

18 being darkened in their understanding, excluded from the life of God because of the ignorance that is in them, because of the hardness of their heart;

19 and they, having become callous, have given themselves over to sensuality for the practice of every kind of impurity with greediness.

20 But you did not learn Christ in this way,

21 if indeed you have heard Him and have been taught in Him, just as truth is in Jesus,

22 that, in reference to your former manner of life, you lay aside the old self, which is being corrupted in accordance with the lusts of deceit,

23 and that you be renewed in the spirit of your mind,

24 and put on the new self, which in the likeness of God has been created in righteousness and holiness of the truth.

DISCUSS with your GROUP or PONDER on your own . . .

What is the danger of not growing up? What can "get you"?

How do Gentiles walk? Why is this dangerous?

How are those who "have heard Him and have been taught in Him" to walk?

How are we renewed?

ONE STEP FURTHER:

Another Prayer

If you have extra time this week, take a look at another one of Paul's prayers in Ephesians 3:13-19. What does Paul pray for on behalf of his readers? Record your findings below.

VOICES
HEARING GOD
IN A WORLD OF
IMPOSTORS

Week Seven: **Paul: Walking by the Spirit**

How does a mature follower of Christ differ from a child or a Gentile? Which describes you? Explain.

OBSERVE the TEXT of SCRIPTURE

READ Colossians 2:18-23. **UNDERLINE** everything Paul warns against.

Colossians 2:18-23

18 *Let no one keep defrauding you of your prize by delighting in self-abasement and the worship of the angels, taking his stand on visions he has seen, inflated without cause by his fleshly mind,*

19 *and not holding fast to the head, from whom the entire body, being supplied and held together by the joints and ligaments, grows with a growth which is from God.*

20 *If you have died with Christ to the elementary principles of the world, why, as if you were living in the world, do you submit yourself to decrees, such as,*

21 *"Do not handle, do not taste, do not touch!"*

22 *(which all refer to things destined to perish with use)—in accordance with the commandments and teachings of men?*

23 *These are matters which have, to be sure, the appearance of wisdom in self-made religion and self-abasement and severe treatment of the body, but are of no value against fleshly indulgence.*

DISCUSS with your GROUP or PONDER on your own . . .

What does Paul warn against? What do these fraudulent teachings result from?

Why do they appeal? What are they worth?

How can we keep from being defrauded?

OBSERVE the TEXT of SCRIPTURE

READ Galatians 1:6-9. **MARK** every instance of *accursed*.

Galatians 1:6-9

6 *I am amazed that you are so quickly deserting Him who called you by the grace of Christ, for a different gospel;*

7 *which is really not another; only there are some who are disturbing you and want to distort the gospel of Christ.*

8 *But even if we, or an angel from heaven, should preach to you a gospel contrary to what we have preached to you, he is to be accursed!*

9 *As we have said before, so I say again now, if any man is preaching to you a gospel contrary to what you received, he is to be accursed!*

DISCUSS with your GROUP or PONDER on your own . . .

What is threatening the Galatian church? How seriously does Paul take the threat? Explain.

Why does Paul say even "an angel from heaven" can be a danger? From the text, what exactly is the danger?

According to Paul, what alone is the norm for truth?

@THE END OF THE DAY . . .

Take some time to look back over what we've studied this week. Then spend some time in prayer asking God to cement to your heart the truths you most need to hold on to this week. Then jot down one or two main points to remember.

ONE STEP FURTHER:

2 Thessalonians
Read this short letter if you have time this week paying close attention to Paul's warnings in chapter 2. Record your findings below.

VOICES
HEARING GOD
IN A WORLD OF
IMPOSTORS

Week Seven: **Paul: Walking by the Spirit**

VOICES
HEARING GOD
IN A WORLD OF
IMPOSTORS

New Testament

140

WEEK EIGHT

He Who Has An Ear, Let Him Hear

"Even so, come, Lord Jesus!"
—Revelation 22:20, KJV

The Apostle John followed Jesus during His entire earthly ministry and is thought to be the only disciple who was not martyred. We know that at one point he was exiled to the isle of Patmos where he wrote the book of Revelation which He received directly from Jesus (1:10ff). Conservative biblical scholarship attributes to John not only the Gospel of John but also 1, 2 and 3 John as well as Revelation.

As we finish out our time together, we'll focus particularly on John's warnings in his first epistle and the words he recorded from Jesus to the churches in the first three chapters of Revelation.

REVIEW

How has God spoken thus far?

In the Old Testament . . . (What was the major shift in Exodus?)

In the Gospels . . .

In Paul's Writings . . .

In Peter's Writings . . .

To Others . . .

John

Since we've already considered the Gospel of John earlier in our study, let's spend some time investigating John's letters. As you read 1 John carefully, note specifically how John says we know God. Also consider if (and how) this differs from what some modern "Christians" sell.

OBSERVE the TEXT of SCRIPTURE

READ 1, 2, and 3 John in your Bible. Then answer the following questions.

DISCUSS with your GROUP or PONDER on your own . . .

Who is the "we" John refers to in chapter 1 of 1 John? How did these people know what they knew?

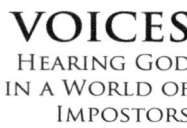

Why is a first-hand witness significant?

What warnings does John give in chapter 2?

What does John say about his readers with regard to the truth? Do they know it?

According to 1 John 2:24, what will cause us to abide in the Son and in the Father?

What specific deceptions does John warn about?

What threat does John warn about in chapter 4?

How can we identify the Spirit of God?

How can we identify the spirit of the antichrist? Why is this important to know today?

Who does "the world" listen to? Why?

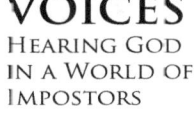

Week Eight: **He Who Has An Ear, Let Him Hear**

Considering the entire book of 1 John, how can a person know that he or she has eternal life? (This would be a great place to make a list!)

What does John warn about in his second letter? How can we be on guard?

SETTING THE SCENE

While the book of Revelation is full of words about visions and voices, our focus will be on Jesus' words through the angel to John in the opening chapters.

OBSERVE the TEXT of SCRIPTURE

READ Revelation 1:1-20. **MARK** every reference to *Jesus* including pronouns.

1 *The Revelation of Jesus Christ, which God gave Him to show to His bond-servants, the things which must soon take place; and He sent and communicated it by His angel to His bond-servant John,*

2 *who testified to the word of God and to the testimony of Jesus Christ, even to all that he saw.*

3 *Blessed is he who reads and those who hear the words of the prophecy, and heed the things which are written in it; for the time is near.*

4 *John to the seven churches that are in Asia: Grace to you and peace, from Him who is and who was and who is to come, and from the seven Spirits who are before His throne,*

5 *and from Jesus Christ, the faithful witness, the firstborn of the dead, and the ruler of the kings of the earth. To Him who loves us and released us from our sins by His blood—*

6 *and He has made us to be a kingdom, priests to His God and Father—to Him be the glory and the dominion forever and ever. Amen.*

7 *BEHOLD, HE IS COMING WITH THE CLOUDS, and every eye will see Him, even those who pierced Him; and all the tribes of the earth will mourn over Him. So it is to be. Amen.*

8 *"I am the Alpha and the Omega," says the Lord God, "who is and who was and who is to come, the Almighty."*

9 *I, John, your brother and fellow partaker in the tribulation and kingdom and perseverance which are in Jesus, was on the island called Patmos because of the word of God and the testimony of Jesus.*

10 *I was in the Spirit on the Lord's day, and I heard behind me a loud voice like the sound of a trumpet,*

11 *saying, "Write in a book what you see, and send it to the seven churches: to Ephesus and to Smyrna and to Pergamum and to Thyatira and to Sardis and to Philadelphia and to Laodicea."*

12 *Then I turned to see the voice that was speaking with me. And having turned I saw seven golden lampstands;*

13 *and in the middle of the lampstands I saw one like a son of man, clothed in a robe reaching to the feet, and girded across His chest with a golden sash.*

14 *His head and His hair were white like white wool, like snow; and His eyes were like a flame of fire.*

15 *His feet were like burnished bronze, when it has been made to glow in a furnace, and His voice was like the sound of many waters.*

16 *In His right hand He held seven stars, and out of His mouth came a sharp two-edged sword; and His face was like the sun shining in its strength.*

17 *When I saw Him, I fell at His feet like a dead man. And He placed His right hand on me, saying, "Do not be afraid; I am the first and the last,*

18 *and the living One; and I was dead, and behold, I am alive forevermore, and I have the keys of death and of Hades.*

19 *"Therefore write the things which you have seen, and the things which are, and the things which will take place after these things.*

20 *"As for the mystery of the seven stars which you saw in My right hand, and the seven golden lampstands: the seven stars are the angels of the seven churches, and the seven lampstands are the seven churches.*

ONE STEP FURTHER:

Word Study: Deceive/Deceiver

If you have some extra time this week, examine the words translated "deceive" and "deceiver" in John's writings. Who and what deceives? Who are the targets? Can we deceive ourselves (see Luke 11:35)? How? Start off with these questions and see what you can discover. Record your findings below.

DISCUSS with your GROUP or PONDER on your own . . .

Who is John and why is he a credible source? Why is he writing?

Where is John and why is he there?

Describe what he hears, sees, and says about Jesus.

How does he respond to the vision?

What is he told to do? Why?

How does this compare with modern-day accounts from people claiming to have heard from Jesus? Explain.

SETTING THE SCENE

Jesus gives John words to write to the churches. As you read, note the true assessments He gives of each community. He doesn't sugar-coat but he doesn't exclude mercy and hope either.

OBSERVE the TEXT of SCRIPTURE

READ Revelation 2:1-7. **UNDERLINE** every negative comment—places where the people fall short. **CIRCLE** every positive one.

Ephesus

1 "To the angel of the church in Ephesus write:

   The One who holds the seven stars in His right hand, the One who walks among the seven golden lampstands, says this:

2 'I know your deeds and your toil and perseverance, and that you cannot tolerate evil men, and you put to the test those who call themselves apostles, and they are not, and you found them to be false;

3 and you have perseverance and have endured for My name's sake, and have not grown weary.

4 'But I have this against you, that you have left your first love.

5 'Therefore remember from where you have fallen, and repent and do the deeds you did at first; or else I am coming to you and will remove your lampstand out of its place—unless you repent.

6 'Yet this you do have, that you hate the deeds of the Nicolaitans, which I also hate.

7 'He who has an ear, let him hear what the Spirit says to the churches. To him who overcomes, I will grant to eat of the tree of life which is in the Paradise of God.'

VOICES
HEARING GOD
IN A WORLD OF
IMPOSTORS

146

New Testament

DISCUSS with your GROUP or PONDER on your own . . .

Negative words:

Postitive words:

Bottom line:

READ Revelation 2:8-11. **UNDERLINE** every negative comment. **CIRCLE** every positive one.

Smyrna

8 "And to the angel of the church in Smyrna write:

The first and the last, who was dead, and has come to life, says this:

9 'I know your tribulation and your poverty (but you are rich), and the blasphemy by those who say they are Jews and are not, but are a synagogue of Satan.

10 Do not fear what you are about to suffer. Behold, the devil is about to cast some of you into prison, so that you will be tested, and you will have tribulation for ten days. Be faithful until death, and I will give you the crown of life.

11 'He who has an ear, let him hear what the Spirit says to the churches. He who overcomes will not be hurt by the second death.'

DISCUSS with your GROUP or PONDER on your own . . .

Negative words:

Postitive words:

Bottom line:

Week Eight: **He Who Has An Ear, Let Him Hear**

READ Revelation 2:12-17. **UNDERLINE** every negative comment. **CIRCLE** every positive one.

Pergamum

12 "And to the angel of the church in Pergamum write:

The One who has the sharp two-edged sword says this:

13 'I know where you dwell, where Satan's throne is; and you hold fast My name, and did not deny My faith even in the days of Antipas, My witness, My faithful one, who was killed among you, where Satan dwells.

14 'But I have a few things against you, because you have there some who hold the teaching of Balaam, who kept teaching Balak to put a stumbling block before the sons of Israel, to eat things sacrificed to idols and to commit acts of immorality.

15 'So you also have some who in the same way hold the teaching of the Nicolaitans.

16 'Therefore repent; or else I am coming to you quickly, and I will make war against them with the sword of My mouth.

17 'He who has an ear, let him hear what the Spirit says to the churches. To him who overcomes, to him I will give some of the hidden manna, and I will give him a white stone, and a new name written on the stone which no one knows but he who receives it.'

DISCUSS with your GROUP or PONDER on your own . . .

Negative words:

Positive words:

Bottom line:

READ Revelation 2:18-29. **UNDERLINE** every negative comment. **CIRCLE** every positive one.

Thyatira

18 "And to the angel of the church in Thyatira write:

The Son of God, who has eyes like a flame of fire, and His feet are like burnished bronze, says this:

19 'I know your deeds, and your love and faith and service and perseverance, and that your deeds of late are greater than at first.

20 'But I have this against you, that you tolerate the woman Jezebel, who calls herself a prophetess, and she teaches and leads My bond-servants astray so that they commit acts of immorality and eat things sacrificed to idols.

21 'I gave her time to repent, and she does not want to repent of her immorality.

22 'Behold, I will throw her on a bed of sickness, and those who commit adultery with her into great tribulation, unless they repent of her deeds.

23 'And I will kill her children with pestilence, and all the churches will know that I am He who searches the minds and hearts; and I will give to each one of you according to your deeds.

24 'But I say to you, the rest who are in Thyatira, who do not hold this teaching, who have not known the deep things of Satan, as they call them—I place no other burden on you.

25 'Nevertheless what you have, hold fast until I come.

26 'He who overcomes, and he who keeps My deeds until the end, TO HIM I WILL GIVE AUTHORITY OVER THE NATIONS;

27 AND HE SHALL RULE THEM WITH A ROD OF IRON, AS THE VESSELS OF THE POTTER ARE BROKEN TO PIECES, as I also have received authority from My Father;

28 and I will give him the morning star.

29 'He who has an ear, let him hear what the Spirit says to the churches.'

DISCUSS with your GROUP or PONDER on your own . . .

Negative words:

Positive words:

Bottom line:

READ Revelation 3:1-6. **UNDERLINE** every negative comment. **CIRCLE** every positive one.

Sardis

1   "To the angel of the church in Sardis write:

   He who has the seven Spirits of God and the seven stars, says this: 'I know your deeds, that you have a name that you are alive, but you are dead.

2   'Wake up, and strengthen the things that remain, which were about to die; for I have not found your deeds completed in the sight of My God.

3   'So remember what you have received and heard; and keep it, and repent. Therefore if you do not wake up, I will come like a thief, and you will not know at what hour I will come to you.

4   'But you have a few people in Sardis who have not soiled their garments; and they will walk with Me in white, for they are worthy.

5   'He who overcomes will thus be clothed in white garments; and I will not erase his name from the book of life, and I will confess his name before My Father and before His angels.

6   'He who has an ear, let him hear what the Spirit says to the churches.'

DISCUSS with your GROUP or PONDER on your own . . .

Negative words:

Positive words:

Bottom line:

READ Revelation 3:7-13. **UNDERLINE** every negative comment. **CIRCLE** every positive one.

Philadelphia

7   "And to the angel of the church in Philadelphia write:

   He who is holy, who is true, who has the key of David, who opens and no one will shut, and who shuts and no one opens, says this:

8   'I know your deeds. Behold, I have put before you an open door which no one can shut, because you have a little power, and have kept My word, and have not denied My name.

9   'Behold, I will cause those of the synagogue of Satan, who say that they are Jews and are not, but lie—I will make them come and bow down at your feet, and make them know that I have loved you.

VOICES
HEARING GOD
IN A WORLD OF
IMPOSTORS

150

New Testament

10 'Because you have kept the word of My perseverance, I also will keep you from the hour of testing, that hour which is about to come upon the whole world, to test those who dwell on the earth.

11 'I am coming quickly; hold fast what you have, so that no one will take your crown.

12 'He who overcomes, I will make him a pillar in the temple of My God, and he will not go out from it anymore; and I will write on him the name of My God, and the name of the city of My God, the new Jerusalem, which comes down out of heaven from My God, and My new name.

13 'He who has an ear, let him hear what the Spirit says to the churches.'

DISCUSS with your GROUP or PONDER on your own . . .

Negative words:

Positive words:

Bottom line:

READ Revelation 3:14-22. **UNDERLINE** every negative comment. **CIRCLE** every positive one.

Laodicea

14 "To the angel of the church in Laodicea write:

The Amen, the faithful and true Witness, the Beginning of the creation of God, says this:

15 'I know your deeds, that you are neither cold nor hot; I wish that you were cold or hot.

16 'So because you are lukewarm, and neither hot nor cold, I will spit you out of My mouth.

17 'Because you say, "I am rich, and have become wealthy, and have need of nothing," and you do not know that you are wretched and miserable and poor and blind and naked,

18 I advise you to buy from Me gold refined by fire so that you may become rich, and white garments so that you may clothe yourself, and that the shame of your nakedness will not be revealed; and eye salve to anoint your eyes so that you may see.

Week Eight: **He Who Has An Ear, Let Him Hear**

19 'Those whom I love, I reprove and discipline; therefore be zealous and repent.

20 'Behold, I stand at the door and knock; if anyone hears My voice and opens the door, I will come in to him and will dine with him, and he with Me.

21 'He who overcomes, I will grant to him to sit down with Me on My throne, as I also overcame and sat down with My Father on His throne.

22 'He who has an ear, let him hear what the Spirit says to the churches.' "

DISCUSS with your GROUP or PONDER on your own . . .

Negative words:

Positive words:

Bottom line:

Looking back over all of Jesus' words to the churches, what types of sins does Jesus call out specifically? Are any of these threats to the church today? Explain.

What behaviors and characteristics in the churches does He commend?

What other commands does Jesus give to the churches?

Do you have ears to hear what Jesus says to the churches? If so, how will you respond?

@THE END OF THE DAY . . .

Oh, there is so much more to consider, so much more to wrestle with and process—enough for a lifetime! Still, over the last eight weeks, we have looked at much. What have been your biggest takeaways from looking at the ways God has spoken through His Word? What are your biggest remaining questions? How will you go about paying closer attention to the voice of God in your life today and everyday?

RESOURCES

Helpful Study Tools

How to Study Your Bible
Eugene, Oregon: Harvest House
Publishers

The New Inductive Study Bible
Eugene, Oregon: Harvest House
Publishers

Logos Bible Software
Available at www.logos.com.

Greek Word Study Tools

Kittel, G., Friedrich, G., & Bromiley,
G.W.
*Theological Dictionary of the New
Testament, Abridged* (also known as
Little Kittel)
Grand Rapids, Michigan: W.B.
Eerdmans Publishing Company

Zodhiates, Spiros
*The Complete Word Study Dictionary:
New Testament*
Chattanooga, Tennessee: AMG
Publishers

Hebrew Word Study Tools

Harris, R.L., Archer, G.L., & Walker,
B.K.
*Theological Wordbook of the Old
Testament* (also known as TWOT)
Chicago, Illinois: Moody Press

Zodhiates, Spiros
*The Complete Word Study Dictionary:
Old Testament*
Chattanooga, Tennessee: AMG
Publishers

General Word Study Tools

Strong, James
*The New Strong's Exhaustive
Concordance of the Bible*
Nashville, Tennessee: Thomas Nelson

Recommended Commentary Sets

Expositor's Bible Commentary
Grand Rapids, Michigan: Zondervan

NIV Application Commentary
Grand Rapids, Michigan: Zondervan

The New American Commentary
Nashville, Tennessee: Broadman and
Holman Publishers

One-Volume Commentary

Carson, D.A., France, R.T., Motyer,
J.A., & Wenham, G.J. Ed.
*New Bible Commentary: 21st Century
Edition*
Downers Grove, Illinois: Inter-Varsity
Press

HOW TO DO AN ONLINE WORD STUDY

For use with www.blueletterbible.org

1. Type in Bible verse. Change the version to NASB. Click the "Search" button.

2. When you arrive at the next screen, click the "TOOLS" button tc the left of your verse. This will open the blue "Interlinear" tab.

3. Click on the Strong's number which is the link to the original word in Greek or Hebrew.

Clicking this number will bring up another screen that will give you a brief definition of the word as well as list every occurrence of the Greek word in the New Testament or Hebrew word in the Old Testament. Before running to the dictionary definition, scan places where this word is used in Scripture and examine the general contexts where it is used.

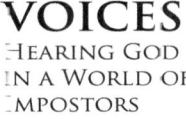

We'd Love to Hear From You!

If you found this study helpful please take

a moment to share your thoughts.

Leave a Review

https://www.pamgillaspieshop.com/products/voices-new-testament

OR

Take a Short Survey

https://bit.ly/VoicesNTBookSurvey